My Sweet Aroma

TIMOTHY GREEN

AuthorHouse™ UK
1663 Liberty Drive
Bloomington, IN 47403 USA
www.authorhouse.co.uk
UK TFN: 0800 0148641 (Toll Free inside the UK)
UK Local: 02036 956322 (+44 20 3695 6322 from outside the UK)

Because of the dynamic nature of the Internet, any web addresses or links contained in
this book may have changed since publication and may no longer be valid. The views
expressed in this work are solely those of the author and do not necessarily reflect the
views of the publisher, and the publisher hereby disclaims any responsibility for them.

Any people depicted in stock imagery provided by Getty Images are models,
and such images are being used for illustrative purposes only.
Certain stock imagery © Getty Images.

This book is printed on acid-free paper.

ISBN: 978-1-6655-9990-0 (sc)
ISBN: 978-1-6655-9989-4 (e)

Print information available on the last page.

Published by AuthorHouse 07/11/2022

authorHOUSE®

Contents

A Beautiful Day

In many ways,
happy and unfazed,
got through the maze,
my babe's celebration.
God's own creation,
a nation of friends
with a love unending.
Away from all the pretence,
No more sitting on the fence.
A lady deserving
slightest signs of birthing.
Our castle, our home, our
palace.

A Beautiful Mind

Foreseen, my lovely one,
courteous and fair,
caused a stir
whenever I am there,
my found hiding place.
Trying to erase me from
memory,
task in the dark my face
explained.

Foretold futures maimed as
you see
but a loving hand drawn
across the pages I scratch,
a match for any talented soul.
From a place older than I,
Sauntered and directly
brilliant,
bereft by those ways I miss.
A beautiful mind, many
hours.
The same way we know
grassland will have its way,
nature will play its part
in regeneration of the heart.

A Day in the Life of Us

A calming and calmed soul,
ready to ride and roll.
Tomorrow not too far away.
For each night and every day,
pleasure, no pressure,
unmeasuring our measure.
A sound of silence and peace,
easing our way through life.
A joyful response,
faithful and true,
my life all settled

with my lady, my petal,
being moulded and grounded
in Christ.

A Prayer for Our Brothers and Sisters in the Faith

However close or far away,

we pray for your safe return

to discern and turn to our
Lord.

Free from the sword and
bought

precious lives to defend,

families to stay bonded to
each other.

The murderers change or fall
by their anger or hate.

Weapons forged against us
shall not prosper.

Lord, we ask for your provision

for our bodies, whether
broken or dismembered;

fortune to follow us always,

Christians truly portrayed in

films and letters, records, and
dates

to remember what was done

at no loss.

A Sign

Signing for me and you,

noticed moments gathered
around.

Wear the crown all over town.

Sunset to sunrise, no fear
found.

Bound not to sin and ready,

ready for action when need be.

Somehow collecting from the
tree,

its leaves heal and feel.

Tenderly she goes until
vanished.

Water replenished and
finished.

Blessings to our bodies and
souls,

harmony felt out of control.

Never fallen, we learn our
lesson.

Glossy hair and feathers
adorned.

Is this a sign from our Father,
our Lord?

Rather be adored for softness

than be respected for
leadership.

Learning from the best,

he beats the drum and sings.
Blossoms come slow and fast.
Not to worry about the past.
Sign of things to come about,
clouds are rolling, flocking,
moving.
The earth is warm to smoulder.
We get older and bolder—
my race, my battle, my time.

A Soldier's Finished Work

Judges and brings light.
Everywhere he goes brings
a sample of a song to sing.
A real soldier born of Christ
fathoms a payment not of
gold.
Feeling his way through the
woods,
he bursts into song along the
river.
Wet and burly I found a way.
Waves wash us clear,
giving its taste to the love we
need.
Breeding until the final
curtain,
new generations of hope and
wonder

began quietly under the sheets,
making his way to his home.
Retreating after a long break,
retirement looms; let's all eat
cake.
Freedom within freedom of
sight.
I know how the world works.
Blind but having eyes to see,
Needing our reach,
easing those troubled minds.

A Thousand Days of Love

Searching to find a timeless
wonder.
Pondering on our past
affliction
made whole out of adoration,
past and present restoration.
Praise his name for
retribution.
Musing and flowing ideas
and ideals.
Kneeling down before him,
showing our humility,
touching and caressing our
spirit.
The Holy One, no spot or
blemish,

sent from heaven to complete his work,

came to us out of love.

Purposefully made clean again,

we stand in awe ahead of him.

Blessed we are as we cope with the hurts.

Blurting out words,

swords pierce like a lie.

Confusion and panic arise,

but our Saviour denies the reprise of evil.

Nurturing and searching our hearts,

healing and breathing our names.

Special we are as we are his saints,

beginning with life-giving blood.

Sins dismissed and forgotten,

our begotten Friend, Keeper, and Healer.

Ships tangle, but not our raft.

Seeking to keep her steady,

born of the sea to baptize.

Let's see a massive reprise of Medway

as we turn our hearts to his way.

A Thousand Days

Time has no scale.

A day can be as a thousand

and a thousand as a day.

Lower our pride and begin to pray,

scoping for next pay.

Time is no commodity.

Searching the horizon—

out past the sea born to a mission—

in misery but hopeful.

Sessions for pay to say …

It's what we are thinking.

Yearning for intimacy,

a plan made into fantasy,

man to see his work.

Makes sense when I think about it.

Strange as the day I was born

to a world that doesn't know me.

Even the trees have to ask.

The task completed,

greet my Maker, our love, our Saviour.

Albatross

Rising for another day away,
floating through the air.

'Dance', I said. 'Dance in the air.'

The albatross knows where to go.

Storms arise, rocks taking a blow.

Searching for food below.

Taking its share and learning some bits,

to the air it takes again.

The horizon looks close to them.

Searching for answers and a protector,

mentions changes of the night,

flighty figures in the background,

making little more than silence.

Eggs are safe at home.

Our bird, the albatross, lives on.

Reason and sense seem to go.

Looking after what, she doesn't know.

Faith shown into the light.

No more storms, nights.
Freedom of peace is born.

An Unsolved Mystery

A glittering missus,
unshattered plates,
a final bout of kisses.
Mates made under wraps.
A series of mishaps
found underneath set traps.
The way is dotted.
The plot thickens.
Free, like a bird
released from its cage.
The key somewhat mislaid.

Another Edit

Bits and pieces,
pieces of bits.
Another one laughs;
another one sits.
How can we see
when we are away from the air?
The campaign and champaign are over.

Reality is real.
The final seal
pushes us to witness these.
A call of hope,
one that's achy.
Wake up, young man.
We need an extra hand.
Be not troubled,
not sore, nor rich.
We have a purpose
for you to be here,
needing to wake
from this foggy state.
Came to a decision
to love.
The bride of mine, shy and selective,
murmured the call
to hide in my heart.
Starting to realise
you are not your own,
bought at a cost.
Melodies from the loving heart.

Answers

Soldiers fall into line.
Buskers waiting for time.
As it passes away,
the lonely would say,
'Why believe in life and love?'
Summer starts life.
Fountains of youth
whisper profound truths.
The answers are written
plainly in his Word,
eachtoourownunderstanding.
Sanding down rough wood
to uncover what's beneath,
breathing new life into
our dream state of oasis.

April

Oh, how times have changed
and will continue to,
until the casting's mould
is broken to society's,
for love to say hello.
It's a chance to join or collide.
Since time began,

the softness of his hand
held close like a cup
and readily poured out
into life's earth.
The cast defeated
by a single drop
of our lover's Son,
the Lord Jesus.

Back Home

My love,
back home to my heart.
The lady in my life
soon to call upon
anytime you like.
Whenever you want and
need.
Spreading our love,
like a world wanting our
seed.
Being free from bondage
imposed by many chancers.
Shackles barely work.
Stripped of all control
for our love is to share our
souls.
The Lord beholds our hearts
safe in his love.

Beliefs of the Heart

My darling, what a way to
start.
Pressure gone, a beautiful
face
erased bad memories of
bondage.
Soldiers marching into line
the beat to step to, the march.
Starched shirt, trousers
pressed,
boots as mirrors, brass like new.
The option to love is oh, so
real.
Their steely eyes ready for
the fight.
Stand aside; my ride is inside.
Bullets chipping away the
walls.
So keen to stop it all.
Stand tall, and avoid the fall.
Mauled and maimed all the
same.
Picture frames on standby.
Where is music, art, and stage?
Fought many a battle of low
wage.
Young, aged, and torn by the
storm.

Born out of necessity.

Prayers going up until handed love.

It is our gift to call one from above.

Our dearest partner, the one we love, warm as the Son.

We belong.

Believe

This kite, I bear and guide.

Fine example of where I put my hope.

Riding the skies, ruling the gale.

Searching for someone
to deliver good mail.

Sailing the whirlwind,
looking, finding, hiding.

I light up as I see you.

I believe your face
is well worth looking for
the thawing flowers.

Oh, we talk for hours.

Breathing My Well-Earned Rest

We turn into the day for a purpose

sometimes made surplus to requirements.

Gated protection for our minds.

Made of rock, but not my own.

Deeper into our energy and synergy,

grounded in faith and belief.

Loving my moments of joy.

Breathing a well-earned rest

having flown from branch to branch.

Trees make me see all this.

Bereavement when we are on our knees.

Retrieving our thoughts of who we are.

Fluttering is our hearts' desire.

Found and beheld the sight

of my child, though we all are alight.

My sunniest son, my brightest star,

what we believe is who we are,

purposely at ease and frozen.
Love chosen by his heritage,
breathing and undeterred.

Catch Your Breath

You give and you take
energy broad and far,
closest you can get
to a friend wide and fair.

Driving a range of returns,
the soft, kind wind
burning by air propellers,
forced into action.

No longer close
in some array,
taking another dose
of summer rain.

Seek the truth so near.
Fears of emptiness
geared for a purpose,
sacrifice of life.

Catch your breath,
the ultimate of expression
to live for a friend

and die for your nation.
Hopes for publication.

Chance

By chance I arrived in this place.
Born to be where time cannot erase.
Pace of the city too much to bear.
I was there for a while, smiling.
In sight was my home by chance.
We danced until sunlight came.
Fought fame and fortune.
Ways we pray, exalting him, melt the heart for a warm start.
Never parted even by the waves,
He says, 'I will always be here.
My dear child, how I miss your voice.'
Choices made to rest and nest bring out the best in me.
Danced until I found my wife.
Yes, the future is all so bright.

At night, the hours of rest.

What a mess; we came apart.

Memories to stay, not wanting to stray.

Waiting for the next night together

brought the hand of time so lively.

First hour of meeting they kissed,

sensing a drifting apart at the seams.

Worldly dreams we tend to seek,

not for our romance.

Come to Me

Heavily laden, sore, and broken,

our lovers tend to be outspoken.

Wages come in and go out.

The world at work comes with a shout.

Take us out to the centre of town,

where time moves on without a doubt.

I am here; speak with me.

Come to my house and eat with me.

Searching and finding a new way.

Big job at the end of the day, where we give up and play.

Come into my being, and you can see

the love humanity has for me.

Tough times passed and gone.

The past has been left behind

with just a few trailing memories,

memories that either hurt or build

healing and feeling.

Believing the tender moments

that make us a wholesome remembrance.

we leave the world but can't survive without you.

Personal choices, like brewed fragrance,

linger for a while and then dissipate.

We stay until the clouds catch our breath.

The net draws us in,

But love sets us free.

Crafted to Be a Bondservant

You know whom I am, what
I do,

yet still love me as I do you,

bringing me through the toil
and snare.

Seeing you, Lord, I would
share my smile

to be in heavenly desire.

Coming back from a
plantation, we require

to sing your praise with all
and each.

Crafted me a beautiful
melody.

Slow me, Lord, so I don't get
ahead of me.

Cause and effect, trouble I
reject.

I rejoice with our Lord's name
made high.

He has a name especially
for me.

Designed to be free from
the pit,

no falls we have as you see fit.

Balanced and true in a new
world.

Fortuneless merit, it's all
fine.

Troubles we do decline.

Blind man or deaf,
your words carried him.

Crimson Dawn

End of the day,
you paint a crimson tide.

Its colours overlap,

weighted in the moonlight,

looking for the final
brushstroke.

End of the day,
larks make their final calls

until the morning.

when we wake,

seeing what the doves see—
a brilliant light
and the misty exterior.

How familiar!

My end to the day
happens when I feel aground.

The way out is to fly in my
dreams,

searching,   finding,
breathing.

Seems strong and holds tight,
trying with all my might
to have rest and settle.

Another battle but always
strong.
I have my Father,
who keeps me from all wrong.
My Father, my protector, my
strength,
my witness, my shield, my
corrector,
my manners, my softness, my
quill.
I see you everywhere.
I shall call out to you.
Oh yes, I will.
Be still, we know your mind.
Handsome fellow,
and oh, so kind.
Unwinding   under   the
crimson dawn,
mixed in colour.
You sure know how to shine.
I am yours, and you are mine.
Sunshine to my days,
moonlight in my dreams.

Deserted but Home

Thought I had a home,
Deserted and alone.
Bring to me my cup.
Sipping with intension,
Breaking the bread.
He always has a mention.
It's a fair trial.
Breathing with intent to live.
What must I show?
How much to give?
Forgetting my chances
To bring out the best.
Full of pure blood and water,
His soul never falters.
Slipping and not falling,
Adoring fans waiting,
Anticipating the sight
Of heavenly power and
might.
Cries but not beaten.
Seated at his right hand,
Even territories, such a great
plan.

Divine Rights

Supernatural beings in authority,

take our rights and free them.

Free from the teeth that chomps at the bit,

pulling, tugging, grappling, grabbing.

Your rights are not meant to be taken

or shaken out of your midst,

sampling what is not free to take.

No mistaking the ways of the world,

where it is all about them.

Pearls are treasured over humanity.

Time to show how it is meant to be.

We have our divine rights to life.

Divine rights to keep,

keep at it, and keep winning.

Your time is here, and more than just singing.

Prizing away the power of darkness.

Indeed, the grubby little fingers slip.

Our Lord, our keeper and Saviour,

will not let us go into darkness where there is gnashing of teeth.

We are harnessed and safe,

No slip, and you carry our weight.

Beloved, keen you are

for the beauty that rises in you

to become health to others.

Hope and faith instilled as our divine rights,

righteous in effect and thoughtful in planning.

Plans that become a glorious reality

Dreams of Home

Slowly we wait
for the freight to arrive.
Always by my side,
never needing to hide.
Sunset, sunrise,
I see my dreams
in your eyes.
Hope of happily ever after,
the missus, the master.

Trains arriving at our stop.
A little step, a hop, a bounce.
Every ounce of strength,
length, and breadth.
A hen, a nest,
newborns are safe.

Dry

Penniless and dry,
poor in man's eyes.
The blind and the lame
all together again,
certain to bring
the birdsong to sing.
Needy but real,
certainly heals the sick—
as the church sees fit—
brought before him.

But the Spirit made man
real,
sealed in the heavens.
Present silences glisten in
the rain.
Brilliance unfolds him.
The lamp beholds his eyes,
wanting and finding all the
answers.

The fight is my Father's.
We won't fall;
we will not be broken.

Dreams and promises awaken,
soaked in glory and honour.
Dripped with blood and pain,
but our Jesus being free
to reign.

Entrée

Entered into a phase.
nothin' there, all erased.
Our Lord we praise
as our souls are raised.
Seems as though we ran dry.
Just as it is; don't know why.
Trying to paint a pretty
picture.
Our Father, always with you.
We try to create as our lovers do.
My, oh my, what a scene,
picture-perfect and green,
bursting nature onto the city
streets paved with life.
A life we don't see at night.
Putting up a fight for the
right,

a right to live and be.
See the waves on the sea,
tossing and turning the water.
Sought a new chapter.
Every second there is change.

Escape

No time to overlap.
We are patient and ready
to beat the demand.
Ride and keep steady.
Ready for the fight.
Survived the plight
of a night of issues
brought to my attention.
Bring me my love and my shield,
and restore my youth,
growth, and strength.
A fight for my heart,
my mind to be one of a kind.
Be my ride inside your mind.
Brought a treasure.
You are no longer blind.
Out of the trap,
made my escape.

Such dynasty, such strength.
Length of days,
enough for endless praise.

Everlasting Joy

The fountain of youth deploys
all talent and blessed hope,
secrets lasting through ages
renewed from pages unexposed.
Joys we understand, oh, so well.
With the everlasting promise,
our covenants with the Lord,
riches of hearts free,
untamed, and passionate
explained unto our souls.
The gentle surroundings
protection of our love.
A soul of strength
towering above us.
But in his humility,
a gentle and graceful smile.

Exercise Your Rights

You have a right to live and
breathe.

You have a right to cry on my
sleeve.

Your rights will not be robbed

because you are robed in
white.

Rights are there for the
freedom of man.

Tested and tried, I hope you
understand.

In times of dissention and
noise,

giving us love to make the
right choice.

Come into my being.

My world is lovely.

Come into my presence.

There you will find rest.

Strengthen your heart.

Exercise your strength.

You have a right to be yourself.

Yourself you know well,

choice and occasion.

Come and tell me a story

of the glorious name.

The one who saves

blood on his brow

believed in us,
somehow came through for us.

Player

You can reach for the sky,

or you can reach for your bow.

The choice is yours.

You can sweep the ground

or turn your life upside
down.

Once again, it's your choice.

Families gather to love and
share.

Beware the fog that lays a
carpet

all over the celebrations,

mopping up the aftermath.

Taken from the city

to find a pitiful piece of land

where passers-by bring sand

rather than something you
can hold.

Bold enough to ask for more.

The shore washing up to the
waist.

Leaving town to find another,

another shop door; poor in
hand

but rich in other ways,
lay the garden flat
as we cover the sand.
Brittle lives and hard times,
we pray for better lives
coming fresh from lines in
the snow.

Father, I Try

Skies sewn from danger.
Oh, cumbersome rain clouds
clouding my vision, systems
drawing closer to you
every day.
Porcelain beauty braves
the sun.
Pockets of kindly king's gold
treasures hidden, but I see
them.
I feel there a sigh of relief.
Father, I do try to tell you
of the fear of telling my
transgressions.
Measured lessons grow solid.
But the Lord sees me as soft.
My words are kind and gentle.
Nature as warm as the sun.

Brought a handsome one
home.
I was turned, tossed, pushed
aside.
My horse taken for a ride;
not a better one in sight
as I go into the sunset.
My God, my love, my all.

Feel

It's real when we open the
seal.
Meals persuading lovers to
feel.
Because we belong to a
different home,
sometimes the tone is ill,
filling each and every void,
employed to bring fresh ideas.
Near every side there is light
Uniting, seeing the sights
delight,
using all his might to free us.
Gallant, brave, fighting for
our souls,
our friend, our brother,
father, and kin,
removing us from the pain
of sin,

timing right at the beginning.
Sifting salt and grainy sand,
panning from side to side.
Taken for an exciting ride,
stopping and starting, drops
weight,
in a state but elated in
opinions.
Dominion overruled the plot,
state of affairs at the time.
The grime and dirt stops;
clean as a whistle we are.
Starting to take up the line.
Divine summer with a
stunner.
Taught to love our lives.
Peace that overcomes fear.

Figure Me Out

A bout of pleasure
temporarily felt.
Hearts breathing and melting.
It's a feeling oh so dear to me.
Answers we find measureless.
Fearing the worst,
expecting the best,
all out of pleasure.

It is a warm, homey, little
nest.
Not to detest or undress the
facts
brought forward to straighten
the hardest of tasks.
Chemical warfare they taught.
The mask we carry,
a new name by contrast.
No longer hiding,
biding his time to hurt and
destroy.
'No', I say. Then I pray to my
healer,
Finding out ways to fight,
reminded of favour, my Lord,
my saviour.
At pace, we bring a way to
sing
heartfelt promises, perfect
timing.
My love from above.
My soldier to bear.
Bearing the weight,
otherwise we would be in a
sorry state.
My Father, Brother, mate.
Yeah, I eat what is there,
almost there.

Find Me a Part

Cause for dissolution.
Bruised into confusion.
Confidence made whole
in search of a home.
Busting out of jail.
Retrieve some lost male.

Find me a part in the book
where I stumble into paradise,
meeting interesting souls,
permeated through the hours.
Powerful forces in trail.
Pen and paper, we write
and see,
seeing our stories unfold.

Tossing and turning,
onwards to the horizon,
where children play,
and their parents watch.
Come into my room,
where there is plenty of it.
Such a rudder for such a ship,
fitting in perfectly
to the edge of the sea,
where the sky follows me.

Certainly we learn to discern
fortune speaks of nothing
when love is what you feel,
kneeling beside my heart,
starting to find a part.

Finding Favour

Savour our Saviour,
he tastes so sweet.
Take time to learn him.
His soul is unique.
Not one drip of blood wasted,
bled for each and every sin.
A crown placed upon him,
in majesty bestowed.
The forlorn maker
took all our pain,
shaking the earth.
Not a grain is lost
feeding our children.

The First and Last

Don't let the world crush you,
your youthful exuberance,
task of standing ground.

Make a stance of solidarity.
The first letter of love,
the last letter of obedience.
Trees form out of passion,
the passion to abide within.
Inside the heart a written letter.
Something of an oddity
muscled out by a last letter.
The odd fashion of advance
made oddly fashionable.
My first, my last, my all.

First Sight

Bring me my cup and saucer,
but nothing slaughtered.
Raise me a crop.
Tend to my daughter;
forlorn and frozen is she.
Bring her love to me.
Share the tears and joys.
Fickle boys used by toys.
Lanarkshire, our dream and home.
Wanting our own place.
Our marriage binding by grace.
Faces never erased.

Driven by our desire to sweep.
Tears and farewell
to our English garden,
and hello to wisdom, our home.
Back on the stage
to marry our own.
Forcibly, talent lies within.
The sense of our peace.
Daily stories to begin

Forgotten

The family I used to share
no more drifts in my care,
drifts away strangely, suddenly
drawn from the well.
Hopefully
brought back to life I dwell,
inserts close to my bosom.
Troublesome, tired, travelling
globetrotters' new home,
felt as though they knew
the path made over time.
Opened by our Lord, our Saviour.
Shown the deepest truths

adventure doesn't always bring.

Singing forgotten and lonely.

Be my one and only song.

You know what once was forgotten

taught me to wait in patience.

Form

Other forms of salvation—
of which we have many—
false teachings supply.
Jesus is the only way.
Sinners deeming themselves
free to voice opinions,
free to hide and lie.
Our Lord is their salvation.
We know true freedom,
freedom from sin.
Pure minds, calm, collected,
controlling our tongues,
escaping war and confrontation.
We see our beauty of many.
Survival is the main goal.
But living is ours.
Holy is our Lord.
Perfect.

Forming Our Space

Who could replace the sail, the face;

souls turning into our fleshly parts;

forming our space away from disgrace;

our places, our homes, our cities, abodes?

Bride nervously unknowing

all she had knowingly flowing,

glowing and growing in faith,

sapped in energy by his taste.

Parts of our hearts and souls

belong to the lover of growth

out of plightful deepenings

followed by insightful fillings.

Filing away the key of our Master

until the days when it is needed.

Plastering the walls and falls

belonging to our safely considered

ground crew, open up so soft.

My heir is here, waiting.

Spaces frequently filled.

Found

We think we have it all
owed us by the world.
Pearls of the seas
rising as we breathe.
Instead, we have found
a blessed town named ours.
Palms healthy,
uncovered like jewels.
But in a sense, the rituals
are no more than empty.
We live by faith,
not by sight.
The watcher of the day and
nights,
safe in the knowledge
our prayers collected,
kept, and reasoned.

Fresh Waves

Tenderly, she awaits her man.
The waves stroking her body.
Sand encroaching her hair.
It is that time of day again,
going home to an empty house.
Fresh waves quiet as a mouse

brought her into peace to
increase.
My feet on the cold, wet sand
brought to me by my own
loving father.
Rather bold to wait for the
tide.
On that slippery ride for a
slide.
Saddled now on the rocky
part,
in the grainy, rocky, and silty
path.
Is it enough to call it art?
Is it enough to say I am a part
of him?
Pain-free, empty of sin, we
can begin,
begin a new story of morning
glory.
Seeking the humble not to
stumble.
Short shorts, baggy pockets,
stopped the awaiting animals.
For a while, it all seemed
well.
Final curtains still the creek.
Creeking shall misshapen.
In the distance he comes to
face
plans to work for good and
embrace.

Final words to share our futures,

murmurs and murmuring.

He sings her final tune as she waves.

General at Sea

Fortune tells me of each and every gain.

Turning up the pressure only gives us pain.

Searching and finding, anchor laid at sea.

Come over, and we shall be with thee.

Important it is to sleep and show

all those individuals who reap and sow

coming together, oh, what a show.

Calm perseverance and a strong grip

turning towards sunset.

My ship, my journey, my captain,

giving us the calm pretence of security.

Waves who wave until the next one gives in.

My love, who are you but yourself?

When we meet, I shall give you myself

when we find your answer to his question,

partaking in communion,

dropping the ammunition,

and pardoned into fruition.

My hope, my peace, my love to increase,

never ceasing to look and to find

the One who calms and secures my mind.

Yardarms stood strong and firm.

Sails filled with its everlasting song,

hull gliding and sometimes jumping.

We can see the horizon.

It's there, right there in front of you.

The Word, my dear, tell me, is it true?

Armed with readiness to journey and awake,

necessity is brought before this world.

And it is necessity that holds us back.

Pull up the anchor, and let's go
back to the home we call our own.

Grace Covering

The sky and its delight
sundry, just like our reason,
flurried, tossed, pulled.
The gifted and broke
yoked in season.
Teased and tainted,
ever present but unusual.
Guardians' guidance
strong, but not highly strung,
there until it is finished
fishing out the dross.
Leaving in place a people
delivered from sin,
a people of love,
all who live within us.

Guards and Nurses
Forerunners busting a gut,
trying to make their way.
Trapped by dust and smut,
searching for a long stay.
Prison or hospital?

It's an easy choice to make.
Brutal dehumanization,
key carriers lie in wait.
The clash, the call.
Guards rushing in,
sentenced and killed,
though no sin committed.
Away with the call.
Echoes beating the walls.
Lives turned around.
Sounds of each triumph
bustin' down the door.
Jail or hospital?
It's built for you.
If the call comes,
be ready for the jumps,
bumps, and scars.
Reputations marred.
Come home and rest.
A new voice comes through:
'You can do it, you know.
Hospital beds
resting our souls.
We may be aged,
but we are not old.'

Tense
Present and past,
feeling it inside.

Strangely, she asks,
'Who is by your side?'
Coming up close,
gliding above the clouds.
Life on ice,
frozen in time.
Life in black and white,
but now I'm in colour.
The progress is clear.
Be calm, my dear.
Clearing the way,
no more smell or decay.
Lighter than a breathless wind,
on eagles' wings,
we see everything.
My food is my spirit,
the Lord my shelter.
Spring is my colour.
Jumping at orders,
not far to go.
We are near the border.
To freedom we go.

Love Reigns

It's the survivor in me
that chooses to strain,
coming in circles.
What is my name?
Refrain from sleep,

keeping on guard.
Beep, beep, beep.
The watch gives it away,
position and place.
You're fast,
so run the race
past struggles.
Scarred in action,
war hurts.
Factions plead for freedom,
painless deaths,
searching for comfort.
Rested until tomorrow,
fix me up.
Afraid of death,
tenderness comes.
Love gets us through.

Give Up

Talk of fight, of war and cries
battled to battle.
Let go and go.
An invisible fort;
forces to protect.
I caught my father
at his drunken state.
Pulled us apart.
Menu of a tough meat
would be me silly.

If left to carry on,

a personal righteous path I took,

far away from the bruise of his nook.

Parts apart at the seams,

no longer roadworthy.

Worn and tired,

take your well earned rest.

Now you are retired,

No war, no fight.

My love, my rights,

simply imply

it's not for me,

this tug of war.

Keen to see

what I'm searching for,

past and present alms,

no more war.

13/80814

Guernsey

Guernsey, bursting at the seams.

Such is the air of mystique.

Having never explored you,

never touched you with my fingers,

I shudder to think where you have been.

When you bring it all with you,

including the kitchen sink,

brought into disregard,

hard to bear you

when all I do is think of you.

All the time I think of you,

unwinding and loosening

the tap, dripping such as the release of your thoughts.

Hardly Fought Daylight

Most of the signs we mindly give.

Bodily massed treasure to live.

Days are broken up into pieces, times for a love's descendants.

Essentially a mass bringing remembrance.

Attendants attending to retrieve.

The daylight often perceived, believed as day brings much more.

Stores full till their very opening,

and it was a very glad opening.

Our sights saw the polite gentleman,

heaven-sent, the One who loves.

Protectors, a glove in hand.

Cold walls rubbed in sand.

We fought for freedom, spending ours.

My colours delivering divine powers.

The night is over; day is sprung.

Brightest passages of new ages, days become one.

Heart's Revival

It's the heart's new birth,
Bending but not breaking.
Our Lord always mending the bridge,
the bridge to our Father.
For us, it is all about the Son.
The sky cannot hold him captive.

Captivating and standing for reason,

brought up for a charge of treason.

Prisoners cannot hold the soldiers of Christ.

Looking paler, whiter but wiser

than any of us could be.

Blood, sweat, tears of years gone by.

Revival pours out to this place,

something time cannot erase.

Praise his holy name and magnificence.

Calmly, freedom shows itself,

kept inside and in good health.

Brought before our Father,

a wealth of knowledge.

Beating founding hearts'

history proves itself to be

another lesson for those who see,

seeking to know the man off the tree.

Searching, finding our Lord, whom we are.

Journeys near and far away,

displaying such courage.

In richness and poor standing,
our hopes are alive, and we
search.
The heart's revival is here.

Her Palette

Secrets of her box,
untainted and untouched.
In the mirror she waits
for the right time,
destiny's door unlocked.
Waited and waiting.
The clock ticks continuously;
every tick gets closer.
The treasure is with her,
staring back from the mirror.
Brimming and simmering
ideas,
unclassified rims of spectacles,
removed for curtsey.
touched her face oh, so softly.
Poised at her mirror as a
canvas,
quickly forgetting the look.
Face glowing in anticipation,
starting with gentle, careful
strokes
invoking confidence.

But unlike the make-up,
It stays with her.

Hey, Sugar, Come on Over

Jumped up and tailored to
suit,
forensics tell me I'm wrong.
Birds causing a stir up there,
nests to craft a home.
Searching and carousing a
mate.
Stately homes rough of state,
Stuff to meet but not to greet.
Families eat and are satisfied.
Fried escallops, tender
dressings—
oh, what a feast, enough to
dress in.
Brilliant news to work and
make.
Enough to scoff that lovely
cake.
Cause and effect, slight but
direct.
Tossed to and fro,
stalled in their efforts.
Wet, hungry, cold.
Set in blue diamond eyes,
surrounded in hope,

causing a torrent of wishes
flowing through the day.
Effective in this time.
Decayed linen replaced,
new cloth and a new place.
Growing up in a family.

His Land

Language so broad and wide,
it's what's inside that counts.
The humdrum of activity
shortened by the day of age.
Every page, word, and deed
brings us closer to him.
Meeting him, oh, what a treat!
Needing his love and strength,
his land deters not a soul.
Old land, sand that awaits not.
The world that thanks our Saviour
would be a great world indeed,
meeting our kinfolk in need.
Breadth and depth sow the seeds.
To see brings life and vigour.
The time and distance of brilliance
take us where we want to be.

Certainty awaits; using our key,
entrance and deliverance we seek.
Brings us a world unknown to them.
Beginnings start with a pounding heart.
His way we don't betray.
No flatteries' radiance stopped.
The plot that opens our secrets,
not to destroy or make shame,
but to agree and make known
lands grown and known to us.

His Strong Arm

Holding on, being strong.
the righteous birdsong.
Come to me, all you weary.
Both simple and wise,
in my nest you can hide.
Living under my watch,
my wings shall carry
you away from every prey,
keeping you safe
night and day,
I shall parry your fears.

You can marry your vows.
No sweet kiss will you miss.
A blessing of many,
my faith I shall give you,
keeping you safe all life through.

Holding On to His Hope

Hopeful smiling lambs,
no wolves to hear our plans.
Doors open for our joys
but close to damage.
Hearts replenished through rest.
Nests made from twigs.
Feeding free to bring
figs born in the rain,
the Son taking away the pain.
Forests, protectors of the world.
I do so protest the damage
caused by mass greed.
But we are abundant,
blessings of hope
without strife or plunder.

Home

I know a place.
The birds sing in unison.
Memoirs out of concept,
nurtured and solid as a rock,
accepting his ways.
Love under grace.
Knowing, all-knowing,
surpassing greatness,
fortitude, safety.
Memories that break me.
Such infall and entrail,
Stirring and stabbing.
My Saviour saves me
from the pit.
Tough as they come.
Gentle as he is,
dressed in glory,
brings me home
to a place called by my Father,
my precious protector,
lover, and friend.

How to Reveal Ourselves

We received what we know,

a certainty like we feel.

But what about what we don't say

and what we don't feel?

Times when we were ill?

A sign of a new settlement

mentions our new discipleship.

Necessary to a new member,

our precious church at home,

groups we call our own comfort.

Nervously we mention our pasts,

thoughtfully ponder our futures.

In our spirits we reveal hidden truths,

granted us a pretence of captive

native oppressors and testers.

Tasted what we feel below,

belonging to a family, a nation.

Posing the question of how:

How and when do we grow?

I Council You

I teach in the best way.

Thinking is for our visions.

Listening is for our souls.

Ways we learn

to love and discern

our strengths, powers,

malleable to his ways.

For in such ways we see blessings,

blessings made for our hearts and souls.

Finding new ways

to live and get by.

I Saw the Sea

'Twas a while ago since I was young,

where the air sang my precious song.

Glorious in waiting, no panic.

Symphonies surrender to it.

Before the Lord we see elegance.

Intelligence forebode the waves.

Years had passed since their union.

Selective is taste into fruition.

I found a place I could feel,

where you could eat a pleasant meal.

Searching for answers on the way,

I saw a stray that lived for today.

I saw the waves brought to me,

centred on the sandy shores,

you wanted more of him.

Grace follows the pace of him.

First, steady, ready.

The light we see is home.

Such a lovely dress.

Send before the Lord-brought gift.

Pattering and flattering,

does it really matter to me?

Certain ways of centred praise.

Amazed at the thought of you,

young and brings me love and joy.

Blessed my love with girl and boy.

Sought-after laughter begins,

trying our best not to sin.

Now we can build up from within.

Ideal Date

We found a place

time cannot erase.

Look in the mirror.

I see your face;

no one shall not deface.

Brought to glory,

worthy of praise,

protected in a case,

a maze of possibility,

keep me on my toes,

remove all my foes

because tonight I rose

with a purpose.

Nurturing my wondering friend,

a joy that will never end,

Not wanting to curve or bend.

Get ready for the weekend.

Not to pretend

but to follow.

In the Divine

My future, my dear, is worth every year.

Your thoughts and your goals

unfolded within us,
beckoning for the call to end it all.
In the divine we pray
to keep it this way.
Partaking of the way you see,
perfectly balanced objectives.
Subjected to fear and pain,
regained after restraint,
the healthy scarred mind.
Cruelty is a terrible thing.
Fears of broken bones,
a death so severe.
Scared but not defeated
by inhuman acts of torture.
Forced to carry those thoughts,
the ones that paralyse.
It is a sad thing when you have two choices—
fight and stay, or give up and go.
Times to remember
extremities of bodies dismembered.
Bonded to the bed,
torn clothes and a heavy dizzy head,
high blood pressure,
heavy sedatives making a mind foggy

and suddenly asleep.
Forgot.

In Waiting

In hesitating,
my lover entwined.
Don't break me.
The heart pulling strings,
the Saviour singing songs,
a fountain of youth
where youngsters play.
Most get old someday,
but not us.
My son, I know you.
Troubles I brought you through.
Your best years are ahead,
so forget past regrets.
Holding you in our loving ways,
don't sweat.

Layers of Love

My layers, filled with air,
made of fire,
my lover, my desire,

crowds do see
your beauty left in me.
I feel you, I see you,
needing your strong love
and company.
The company I thrive on and
need.
The warm land
giving up its fruit in season.
You are made for a reason.
My blossom and a colourless day,
the heart that gives
the ability to pray.

Life after Marriage

Promises to carry,
sharing the blessings
and the burdens
to say yes
through the fire and rain
untouched.
The Son amidst
any weather,
shoeless and toeless,
small or large measures,
rations and irrational,
reacting to catch you

whether in danger or fall.
All these things I pray
to reach out and say,
'I love you, my bride, my friend.'

Bringer of Light

The battle is won.
Coming out of all angles,
angels rejoicing at the sight
of our rich lives
from rags to riches.
Many find shelter,
hiding under his wings,
and into your arms
feeling relief.
Ordained to serve,
we deserve to live
lives dedicated to serve.
Unnerving moments do pass,
surpassing greatness
as we bring new
understanding,
motions, and emotions
clouding the space
between us.
The closer we live,

beginning to find
the light we yearn for,
is ours to share,
becoming our minds
always there.

Little One, Don't Cry

Turning your head
as he lays down to cry,
the sadness invoked.
My, oh my, why do I do this?
Printed each page for a kiss.
His mystery and history,
stories of sailors washed up,
wives, daughters reunited,
softly sighted, eyes backed up.
Brought into each moment
fragments for memories' sake.
Forgotten by our friends,
close ones we feel for
do draw us in for a while
tucked into our blankets.
Freedom to sleep in comfort,
I remember you as then.

Lots

Our Saviour's mind to bring us
together as his bride,
certain apprehensions we feel
when we talk of eternity.

Derelict and unconscious
by way of design,
tried and tested ways
brought faith in thine will.

Happily, we take the step of
faith.
Colours certain
due to current concern
of tripping.
Case of change or chance?

Burdened with the dullness,
our ways are alien to see
the candid force of forever be
searching and finding.

Lots cast on our Saviour's
clothes,
but not the ones he now wears.
Minds of their new owners
did what they were sure of,

but at his death, minds were changed

as our Saviour, heroic to the letter.

Chance happens.

We put our chances and hopes in him,

certain to see even as eyes grow dim

love poured out through future, present, and history.

Love's Justice

Forgiven misfits,
metered lines gone.
The sun shines.
Found my paradise,
all safely inside
beside my well,
your story to tell.
When the stars fall,
falling on a land,
the pounding earth,
the split sea.
Home we need for us
as we search deep,
deep inside him.

Love's Actual Truth

The bounty full of love and cares,

never quitting and always there,

ending not the closed curtain lost.

Frosty moments to endure gladly.

Searching and finding for rest.

Oh, sir, not, but forever my best.

Testing resolves all those involved.

In the harrowed nights of retrieve,

left ear cleft and bruised,

a child downtrodden, abused,

feeling used, broken, bemused,

standing and unafraid.

Once were bricks now plundered

through darkness unerred.

Under cosh, body parts lost.

Lock and key could not stop

envelopes sent in danger, in faith.

Precious moments happily wait
till the gates open.

Magdalena

We fit like well-fitted bodies,
coming together like the light
in all its love and essence,
it's brilliance, and it's majesty.
Calling us home to the stars,
where we can live and play
with the clouds we draw our breaths.
The storm is our power.
The winds are our instruments.
The sea our drinks.
Our Lord Jesus is our bread,
bread of life, calling to be savoured.
Another labouring power for our neighbour.
Touch my heart, and feel my soul.
Be bold to know that we wish for your success.
Undress in the mirror
that our bodies are truly blessed,
dressed like the flowers.

Naked lie the trees.
Gusts play with the branches, strong with resolve
against the current state,
suckling on every way we pray.
Searching,
wanting,
flying.
We begin with an inward breath,
crossing from death to life.
So what is next?
The clue is in her name,
pressed with honour.

Mail Coming Home

It is a far cry from where we were,
shaking and shivering
through the night,
suffering in silence,
taught to be mindful.
Step by step, we became lighter.
Light my fire to have my desire.
But we do need rest.

Coming home, the mail gives
love letters from land to sea.
Harmony when received
brought us comfort
that time we needed a smile.
Where are our lives? Where?

Mail finally received.
Desperately felt and misspelt.
It is the reason and not the way.
Praying   for   tomorrow's
kindness.
Waves watch the boat,
rubbing, gushing, crashing.
It sees the erosion,
erosion of lives washing by.

Plots to destroy were denied.
It's a case of let's run and hide.
We know our hiding place—
under the wings of our Father.
Rather than us fighting,
he fights for us,
trusting his protection.

Man Born at Home

'Twas a tender night at home.
When I was born, I moved.

For a while, I sensed a debate.
Whom have I to share this
cake?
So I was born a man who shares
and always can win our hearts
and minds.
Some force showed my kind
hand.
Landed up on the distant
shores,
fighting for survival and for
life.
Man-made, spirit-inspired,
lovingly crafted from the
purest paint.
Point of place, point of reason,
praising your songs made
real.
The dark is lit up,
pulling   through   our
memories,
distancing the crow from the
dove.
Our love is finished into
brilliance.
The perfect soul who waits.
Food and debates occur,
heartstrings twitching,
pulling at my coat for a voice.

Merrily We Go

Merry little wonders to show
to our brethren to know
how we work and how we play.
The store they watch,
timing the hours, the so-called watch gives.
What is watching? Who is watching?
Why are we watching?
To pass the time?
It is the choice we have to make.
Calmly given, oh, what a way.
Patience calling for slow words.

Merrily we go

further than ever before.
the door lift jammed open
showing and guiding in the way.
Are we here to learn?
Are we here to earn?
Are we here to move?
Are we here to give?

It is almost a positive change
when the ages and aged
show us better ways.
Boldly we go towards
a new beat.
certain to show
sands departing,
war defeated,
and souls gifted.

Miss Fluoxetine

Oh, so lovely, no despair here.
Friends and lovers come to drink,
thinking of thou partial days,
sunrays shining so beautifully.
Damsel waiting for her prince,
a part of him to have and to hold.
Prince so bold as to choose.
No bruised reed he would break
habits that time may erase.
Fewer men of stature to see.
This is a friend I'm sure you will love,

respectful of all their comforts.
Ways of the brotherhood
understood
below the days brought ahead.
Playing with my fluoxetine,
how blessed we are to come
home.
Fought for her hand in
marriage,
being my loving self brought
forward.
Blessed hope, a balanced
meal,
my love not needing to steal.

Moments of Life

Time has its space,
unable to be erased,
such beauty that surrounds us.
Fuss made of so little
belittles me,
and I stop searching.
Moments in our lives,
we stretch the truth at times.
Barely here,
I fear the worst sometimes.
Merely mortal limitation.
Take them on.

I am with you.
Pondered the contempt
of an unjustified exit,
an overcomplicated answer
fancied amongst men.
The tables turn homeward
to the light,
where beauty is treasured,
unmeasured by performance.
Heart lying dormant
beneath the sky.
The moment we wake,
the sun pulls us in.
Yes, the son tugs at my heart,
starts it up
to win the race.
A special prize to be won.

Mount the Mountain

'Twas a great day when I said
goodbye.
In the blink of an eye, she was
gone.
Most pretend it was tough, but
relief was felt inside.
Coming together on one big
ride.

Sheepish but brave, I went home for my rest.

This mountain we face is steep and dangerous.

But in our Father's arms, we feel safe and secure,

belly full and nurtured for further use.

Clearly bruised, bemused, and misused.

Plain to see the ride she was on—

one for the mountain and one for her son.

So the ride was hard; do I dare to tell

of the foxes and vixens there to ensnare?

Minus the two friends who misused you.

Where was your protection or crew?

On wings and in flight, your captain is calling.

Enduring with patience, another dawn is dawning

September was great, so much rest and new friends.

Poured out until empty, and fully we seek his provision.

Sharing the hope, we made ourselves to see

comrades lost to death or decay.

Winter is waging against the summer beams,

showing the snow, it turns up its nose.

Blue sea and sandy shores react and pose.

New island away from it all,

undiscovered escaping free from the tide.

The tide that drowns but gives the land its shape.

Beauty comes and goes from the nape to the toes.

Come over, my dear. Everybody knows

calling the sails to direct us homeward,

pulling and tugging us

until we come clean.

It's freedom, my love.

Know what I mean?

Music in Me

For my sanity, I remembered times of total intimacy.

Music was the format
forming inside my brain.
Total restoration and
regeneration
Hard to believe it is just a
distant memory,
searching and finding a way,
living each day
as if it is your own.
Last appeals for freedom
finding resistance.
Resilience pauses for thought:
What if I get what I want?
Would I be the same
sunny sunshine?
That is me, and I try
to make a sound.
Curling up in a new place,
the place where I can live
and breathe
seated in glory.
What a wonderful truth.
It hurts, the pounding
headache.
Curable with basic tools—
prayer, silence, and peace.
Be at ease, my friends.
Music made in me
external forces made real.
My reality.

My Diary

This world has changed,
too much drama.
Arranged rather oddly,
several pairs of socks.
Worry about odd flavours.
Next of kin, our Saviour.
We are salvaged
from the wreckage.
Messages sent in truth,
holiness, trinity.
Eternal blessings
tried and passed.

My Ears

I hear what I see comfortable
for me.
Breeze coming in from the
rain.
Be careful of what you let in.
Brilliance of a sane made me
smile.
A smile you wish you had
heard,
like a rainbow without song.
Half the ways we perceive,

crashing waves not known.

Vibrations in and for my eardrum. Hitting drum heavily.

I know the song made fresh dovetails silently, making a nest.

Found a place to be right.
Happy girl, such a delight
Trying with all his might,
a doctor to deem fit my sound.
It's who we are that counts.
Money goes to the well-wishers.
'How do you hear?' I must ask.
It's like listening to the sunshine.
The tide will come by.
Feet covered in love
made wet and tears supply.
Abled bodies taught to share.
We feel what's ours.

My Fair Lady

I look upon you, and I wonder
if I serve your needs.
Under our Father's covering,
a lady I love and treasure
above others is a good measure.

I wish to serve you
with warm comfort
of feathers
through all the storms,
keeping you dry.
And I ask why I have you,
and then I am shown
it's a gift
from my Father.

My Famous Follower

Brought to justice,
learning his lesson.
Must have been born
into such distress.
Depression measured thinly,
becoming one place
for us to live in.
Keep on climbing.
You are counted to be
within our family.
Soldier coming home
bearing the scars,
racing hearts dependent
on the words coming
from his heart.
Starting to understand,

understanding the arts.
Counting the stars and pennies
brings plenty to talk of,
why we feel as we do.
Lesson learnt.

My Father's Smile

He gives freely; no need to cry.
Sensing a fall holds us high.
Plentifully wise, the surprise is ours.
Waking, working, and serving,
he leads me to fresh, still waters.
I mute the mule to hear his voice.
Your smile I cannot deny.
The surprise you give me every time.
Dining in the forest restaurant,
bringing home a craft.
Oh, crafty me, what a surprise.
How many eyes see it?
For my happiness longs for it.
Lifting me up, a hint, a glimpse.
A soldier's prerogative to wince.

The winch that pulls us through,
my Lord, my aid, my rescue
feeding on your Word.
Bring the stranger to us.
Beating drum, exhale awhile,
home to a beating heart.

My Freedom, My Choice

The first chance I get
when I am out and about
nurtured talent.
Please send a scout.
My freedom, my choice.
When I come home,
it's because of you I stay.
The home you make us,
the home you maintain,
mountainous tasks
seem little to you.
Keeps me alive
and virtuous too.
Found me in a good place,
where lovers rest.
And to us they gaze,
wondering how to do it.

It is a case of giving.
Not giving in,
but giving of ourselves.
Our fruits of tomorrow
ready to eat at the right time
blessed to our bodies.
Nurtured and clean,
wet and slippery.
The pain comes and goes.
Quickly our toes dip
into the sea of forgetfulness,
casting away all fear and
doubt.
The love we found
free for boundless wonder.
Love, free us from decay.
We want to be as you are
in the spring of May—
fresh, clean, and ready to be
real.
Several places we visit,
but nothing feels better
than coming home.

My Friend

To my loving friend in sight,
never ugly and such a
delight,

the night calls us on high.
Why the face? Are you all
right?
Kissing and then coming
home.
Unknown to us the frosty
moments
sought after lofty surgeons.
Lives lived within
boundaries.
Boundlessagesandadventure.
Measureless properties void,
void of pain and a known
name.
Searching, buying, keeping,
weeping for more choice.
Raise your brow; make a song.
Your voice and opinion
matter.
My friend, I am with you
throughout all the ages.
High or low the wage,
seems like all we want to do,
sailing through the pages.
Age showing itself,
rocky mountains, higher
hills,
frosty windowsills,
chills left.
And now the Son remains.

My Heart and My Love

Dear Lord, we delve deeper,
loving Father, our keeper.
Seeking all you have made,
Purest form and high grade,
making us whole and holy.
What a fortune you give us
to you moving heavenly.
My heart I give and seek
your ways on top of our leaking
wills.
Still you make, still you feel.
For my sake, raking the leaves,
a clearer path so I can walk.
Living words to me you give.
Lights on the soul, you feel
and bring.
May I be so bold and say
to us you bring us this way?
Hence, while I think and
speak,
my mouth wallows.
But my pen is strong.

My Heart's Desire

Butter me up to flutter and
mutter.
Seas swim enough to be
grounded,
Waves waving their
magnificence.
Just the right ambience.

Their moods deter me,
as do the settled way they are
searching for reason.
Girl, you have come so far.

The way you strike the bell,
the way you search for health,
minds moving into shapes.
Fortune and promise await.

Answers too much to bear.
The heart you see,
you can find answers there.
Button me up.

I sing like a canary.
Striving to be one.
Wanting the sea,
but not a drop to be wet.

Feelings occur at any time.
Mastered and plastered,
Much too much wine.
My ear inclined to find
a perpetual prize inside.

My Lady, Lover, and Friend

I have found you at last,
my maiden surpassing hopes.
You love with all your heart.
You have turned my desolate life
into light,
a holy and warm flame.
And my life would be
the same as always
without you.
To bear your tears, pains, hurts, and fears.
To understand what it feels like
to be a loving wife,
to learn your ways,
and to encourage the truths you impart.

My Little Fantasy

My teacher always planned for further negotiations.
Playing dumb, I asked, 'What about carnations?'
Days and times blur into one.
Wanted to control and make me numb.
Searching other ways to pray and to win.
It's our style as we empty the bin,
Lovers talk about gain and loss.
You are my goal, to live, to breathe.
Such a lovely place to be and see.
This wonderful heart of ours, sounding the trumpets.
Angelic rhythms taking us far beyond the normal.

It's our little dream,
Big in our hearts.
Seams being tightened
sings like the lark.
Dark out there, where the crows eat.

We sit on his commands.
Underground worries dispersed.
Nervous tweeks unreversed.
Deserve to live, breathe, and be.
We are all a big family
where dreams are real,
and the trees feel surreal moments.

My Lover, Pure and Holy

Tower of strength,
sure and spotless,
my earthly queen.
My trusted one on the throne.
Together known to call on
soldier and protector,
messenger and guide.
Someone to show my sides.
Open, true, and new,
the one I go to.
Fruitfully multiple gazes,
amazing sights.
Totally besotted lover
belongs to none other than God.

My Message for You

Because you are home and free,
I see your love constantly.
My message for you is this:
Be all you can be,
searching for your answers
deep in my soul.

The best way to know and see
is to belong and feel like you are me.
You are my righteousness,
drawing people from everywhere.
Your heart is my goal.
Your soul is my friend.
We search.

Coming along the road of destiny,
rocks removed before us
work with and in your heart,
starting a place where you will reign.
We are also waiting for the Son to rise.
Caught in a mirror, our eyes meet.

Streets are full of our love.
That's the goal.

Brought from far and wide,
not to turn or hide.
The church, our bride,
come inside, and we will
show you.
Homeward bound for glory,
stories and testimonies
unfold.

My New Sweet Sensation

Emotion, like the ocean,
moved into moving.
You grasp the banister,
needing help.
Tossed and thrown
into the midst of your own
powering through the air.
Solemn and salty breeze
removing all disease.
Fleeting moments of peace.
Pieces scattered and collected,
measured on a scale.
A reliable one of judgement.
Sentimental tides drawing in,
break away from sin.

My Planetary Wish

For years I asked myself why
plants exist in this morbid
state,
pulling and tugging at the
earth,
Feeling a way to survive.
Destitute are values or
wisdom.
Weeds breaking through the
steely surface.
One way to find the path,
instilling a sense of freedom.
Certain to be a witness
to a foggy, relentless existence
bought with presents and
assurances
of a better way, a better day.
Leaves taken from a soup
chewed on,
bruised, battered, broken,
stewed.
The brew making for a moment
of clarity.
Mistaken for a wife,
sitting and waiting.
Indignation seen and heard.
Tarry, carried the heavy load
brought love within itself.

My Run

It's a race, and we're winning,
searching and always finding.
Do I really need reminding
of the colours
that run straight through your hair?

On to victory, my brother.
Lives shift and change.
But change for you is easy.
You craft your entry
perfectly on time.

Sisters are calling me,
searching to me for an answer.
Powering through life,
no handmade raft.
It's my Jesus, my Saviour.

Rather than setting up camp,
you roll with the flutter.
Birds fly in season
years to find a reason
away from the world's prison.

My Teacher

How lovely to hear you,
and I feel hopeful
when you tell us
we please you.
Our fountain of youth
life poured into us all.
At times feeling so small,
faithful for us
the trust you want
for you to bear the brunt.
The hunt for salvation is finished
with a single breath.
Close, like the comfort
of the breast's nest.

My Time

Edging on the sublime of hosts,
bereft of the meaning of love,
life itself captured in a dream.
Oh, heavenly hosts, where have you been?
Circling around time and space,

becoming strength at his will.

Our sign we are safe.

Kept for us outside of time,

his design made ours.

We have arrived right on time.

Found upon our planned planet,

gold exchanged for the carrot.

Marvels at his rich tone,

a voice of love we all own.

Sitting in the park so alone,

my time to sit and ponder

what life out of time means.

Gifting our hearts into keeping.

Our kept hearts retrieved,

a thousand truths believed.

My Will

Henceforth, bring my will

in brilliant white and purer still.

Waves come in, and tides go out.

Fortune passed as I sat and wondered.

Don't squander what God gave you.

Stay well and in the peace of Christ.

Peace be with us we do trust.

Have you still time

between our fruits of labour?

Certainly our fruits are from the Saviour.

We are in the book of life's love,

undeterred strength from above.

Dining in the homes of worship,

gladly paced our tracks of kinship.

The sky rolls in and docks,

moving the homes of the fox.

No one can blot us out.

The king of love casts out all fear.

My friend always near my heart.

No Pain

By chance come our measure,

measured for right fitting.

Splintered and sewn,

the gift of a happy home.

I cupped you in my hand.

The water ran dry,
and your tears turned
upside so we can have joy.
My sweet lady,
swift to look at me,
slow to ring that bell.
The service is great.
My lovely kisses.

Not Broken

They tried; I fought, I thought.
They hunted; I ran, went home.
Father, they ran; I outsmarted them.
Wanted to break me; now I see
how a lover should be
living in peace and harmony,
undeterred in fighting,
feeling at peace in the world.
Some think life is cheap.
We are not for sale.
We have been saved
by the blood of Christ.

Notes for the Judge

Seen my work, and I hope you are well.

Making a movement, but still as a statue

turned on its head and made an example

of the love it takes to sample the sweet, sweet taste of victory.

Victory we feel as the numbers swell up.

Seeing you there makes me well up with emotion.

As the devotion takes a turn,

turning down a one-way street,

dangers creep in from many corners.

Search for the truth, my handsome wanderers.

Today is yours as we flourish in the fields of love,

Ready for the word of acceptance.

On the Surface

It was a big change when I met you,

darling buds of May.

Couldn't change the way we are.

Such tenderness a planet, a star.

On the surface, lacking and bizarre.

Underneath, a shepherd boy,

the heart of a lamb of peace

kept clean and at ease.

No tropical disease to report.

Undistorted, bent, or torn.

Reborn is a youngster today,

Praying for a better place.

Time cannot erase the face.

Sometimes life is such a maze,

chasing the road away.

Sent to bless and nurture,

always going much further.

Taken aback by reality,

meditate, fighting rivalry.

While the surface walls are hard,

underneath, just mortar.

Plans I have for you to grow

nurtured the flock, and we are stopped.

Ancestry

Past times look to the skies.

Importantly, dries our eyes as they cry.

Wisely, we see above the trees meals shared with our peers.

Honey, the sunny proposition, brought forth a whole sense of reason.

No law broken.

We speak of the unspoken, woken to live and serve.

Our ancestry makes our history.

Our future is happily placed with him,

our Lord, Jesus Christ.

The One who came to serve and save.

Certainly sure of our new home,

homey dwellings casted in honour.

Answers follow our character.

Mastery of our gifts to follow.

No more mistakes.

Taken at the very hour of consent,

bursting the banks

of the river on which we were born.

See before me the love of us all.

Falling on our knees, foes defeated.

Our Christ, our Saviour,

keen to pour out his blessings.

Ringing the bells, the sounds awaken.

Oh, see my sweet home.

Our Bread

Kneading and moulding,

forever holding its taste.

Manna from God

smothered in peace

and covered in promises,

cut with precision

and served with a smile.

It is what we need.

It is what we want.

He gives of himself

in hopeful love.

He shares his dreams,

plans to succeed,

feeling our pain,

taking the blame.

Our Father, the risen Lord,

great Redeemer and Comforter.

Our Covering

We stand and train.

Got out at the right time.

The unceremonious dumping,

a dumping ground

for the strays or subconscious.

Raised by our Father,

the words implanted in my brain

by a love so true.

A public spectacle turned.

Our Daily Bread

The bread, our lives

turned upside down.

His mighty hand kneaded

rolled, tinbound, risen.

Saved from waste

that ravages this world.
A remembrance of past lives
whirling around; minds
spinning, flickering, dotting
every sentence withheld
from all pure-hearted souls.
Our Saviour, our King,
best friend, and lover.
The brother we talk with,
the family we would die for.

Our Future Plans

Rather we talk some seasoned
words,
choice words we share aloud.
Never to be diminished are
our values.
Taught to share one's wit,
sauntered and shaped into
perfect fit.
It's still there, gone nowhere.
Gales that cry, winds that
burst.
Colours shaped into drastic
notes.
We find many answers in prose.
The nose drops, its deposit
strangely

made known of a stored page.

Blessings to me you are.
Finding our feet,
we won't change.
The noise nearly shook me.
Screams and shouting not a
good sign.
Purposefully kind to any
stranger.
Growth from birth settled and
real.
Appeals to the courts for
freedom.
Fear and dread fueling their
resistance.
Sought to be free with my
family.
Not deterred from my quest.
Finding a way to leave a
broken home,
not caring of the fuss and
upheaval.
Home I ride and live my
dreams.

Our Plot

Our little piece of home,
striving and wishing

for our own.
The plot, unravelling knots,
just like life.
Sunset to sunrise,
a loving surprise.
Gazing in wonder,
facing our Father,
our little piece of land.
This surface to expand,
lend me another hand.
Pull me up when I am down
to awaken the thawing
ground.

At Thy Service

Your foot-trodden path
straight to my heart,
divine in health.
Love truly melting.
A full understanding,
turning every stone.
Solitude for prayer.
Lord, we're almost there.
Finding a foothold
in a dangerous journey,
the wounds bruised and
confused,

never stopped you.
Feeling for you
as the plot surrenders,
strange places defended.
Grace follows you everywhere.
In tow, many
looking for answers.
The quill controlled the
tongue.
We belong with you,
our fortress, our hideaway.
Your heart, our home

Our Sky's Delight

Pondering for the protection,
delight in right direction.
Pinned onto us a fraction of
the stars.
My sky, my Saviour, my
Flavour
points out my behaviours,
colours.
Both may eat, but the sky
gives,
giving all to those who dream.
The day and night lights
delight
when we conquer our plights.

Fantastic awakenings do wait
until we find our chosen
mates.
The sky sees success
when in attire we do dress,
from our resurgence of energy,
bought and given daily and
grandly.
My hand may slip and bruise.
My body laid down to use.
But my dear, now I am
interested.
Printing our own
masterpieces.
Water flooding the streams.
Seats empty and frozen.
Our lives live in.
The sky survives.

Our Team, Our Rules

He looks up at the sky.
Why does his heart long
for her?
Because she belongs to our
team.
The rules to prolong
our youthful sunrises.
The opposition subdued,

we chant and we sing.
A songbird's call,
calling out in Jesus's name.
Rhythm maintained,
a chant to surrender
all nations and forces.
Enjoy it, my child.
It's all in your smile.

Over the Top

Being sent into war
is a task I would refuse.
Coming of age,
leave out the dirty page.
Useful for the scrap heap.
Seeping in the noise.
pains that disfigure a man's
plan.
Plans to prosper and not harm
are made as a guide.
Keep the light glowing.
Inside, we form each breath,
ones that give you strength.
Nurture the future
to see success in his eyes.
Prize for the winners,
simmers with pride.

Dancing and praising
into the night.

Partly His, Partly Mine

Belonging to a sound mind,
unwinds and then caresses me,
certain to cause a stir.
She is mine, and I am hers.
Fantastic appearances
discover.
A planned rest to recover.
Planted within a gaze,
the maze of a maid's talent
masked beyond the rich
gifts of purity, speech, and
humility.
Humbled before our dear
queen.
My Lord, whom have you
seen?
Believe me, I am keen to
undress.
Fancied folks coming home
to rest.
Time is golden, and words are
thine.
Thrifting through the minds
of the ill,

better still than to hide your
bill.
Toasting a God of love and
mercy
bursting on to the scene
clean, real, seen, and
believed.

Peace of the Saints

Surpassing all colours of my
youth,
my entrant is suffering.
Ways in which we praise his
name
talks for a different purpose,
cleansing and making whole.
Jesus—the way, the light—
discovering we do not need
to fight.
Kindly gives a way for reason
born in a humble fashion.
Come home, my Protector.
The fight is yours.
We just need to wait for the
day he comes back.
Sackcloth worn,
ashes finishing the old ways,
taunted and bare until the
final curtain.

Pertaining to be free
structures form in the minds,
binding the honour that is
ours.
Calling the final hour to
begin,
a trumpeting sound.
Calls and deflections
mention a way of escape.
Feeling no remorse for our
past deeds.
Come in, and be with me.
Eat and be merry
for the time is near.
Coming up from the cold,
saints calling out from
distress.
A totally new address
built of love, sweat, and
tears.
Every day nearer and nearer.
My fractional beliefs add to
naught
as he builds our temple
on holy ground.
Sounds escape, but we are his
bride,
calling and wanting to come
inside.

Personal Growth

Persons of youthful deterrence,
occasional growth occurred.
Sir, why are you here?
This place is deserted.
Before you go on your way,
please come with us to pray.
Fortune is there, and so is loss.
Our lives awaken.
Getting rid of the dross.
Why are you there?
No will or a home?
Sir, I tell you what I have is
not my own.
Fortitude and a pace of Rome,
a soldier am I,
a stately place and position.
The Lord, my protection,
saved me from a section,
position, or pose rags or throws.
This now is my place
through my saving grace.

Let Us Get Personal

Personas meet and clash.
Is there another way?

Sometimes a hash-up?
Were we born this way?

Enchanting oceans rise and
fall.
But the human condition is
level.
Steady we are as we go
homes to homes,
delighted and invited.
Tears of joy we forever see.

Personal kindness watching
and waiting
for our day to arise.
Coming from far and wide,
not missing or hiding a beat.
Closer than our very own
heartbeat.

He comes in such majesty,
calling for history to unwind.
Kindness floating like a kite
in the wind.
Winds can do that.
Winds that shine in the
desert.
Winds that guide us to be level.

Memories taken out of context.
Nesting, a home we wait for.

My persona, white and pale.
All we need is choice.

Pictures

You see me? I'm picture-perfect.
Nervous? Yes, I have been in
neglect.
Happy? The type that is
settled.

Yes, we live and seek
the needs of others.
Covers the dirt, not disturbing
peace.
The soil, the soil perfectly
ready
to find a love made steady.
Bursting with colours and
light.
Delighting in the changes
made fit for all ages.
Playing with hand-built
toys,
Searching for a voice.
Hard to bear the sudden
flare-up.
It's a kind thing to bear.
Atonement and courage,
what does it mean?

When we are discouraged
for beyond our horizons,
plenty to pick.
I have chosen my love.
Walk with me; I shall be your tree.
Fresh in spring,
cool and collected in summer,
wintery gaze, and unfazed by others.
Not an inch closer
than to the desert.
My pictures made to be
a sudden flurry of debate
we see in a state of loving our minds.

Player

You can reach for the sky,
or you can each for your bow.
The choice is yours.
You can sweep the ground
or turn your life upside down.
Once again, it's your choice.
Families gather to love and share.

Beware the fog that lays a carpet
all over the celebrations.
Mopping up the aftermath,
and taken from the city
to find a pitiful piece of land
where passers-by bring sand
rather than something you can hold.
Bold enough to ask for more?
The shore washing up to the waist.
Leaving town to find another,
another shop door; poor in hand,
but rich in other ways.
Lay the garden flat
as we cover the sand.
Brittle lives and hard times,
we pray for better lives
coming fresh from lines in the snow.

Pocket

You are made to serve,
deserve the handmade gift.
Don't bite the hand that feeds.
And all giving proceeds

found on a mountainous path.

The parks look fresh,

with leaves and a soft mesh.

My pocket may be short,

but I fill them.

Every decent soul,

I see you breaking through.

Keep trying, young bandsman.

Your mind is strong,

and you touch gently.

Poems on the Move

You move me, like winter tears,

supporting my sanity and drenching my soul.

Coming together after a brawl,

where all they do is train for war.

My jaded mind seen as dumb.

Sore over time and distance away from home.

Although I have not seen you,

my Lord, I have been with you

on the move; you are with me always.

A shady past now becoming a cool shadow.

Meadows of beauty with narrow paths.

Tasked with a mission, whom do I ask?

Peace be with you, Son.

Jesus

We spin and we teach,

awakening our dreams.

Seems too much to bear.

You sought my heart to start,

beginning to ask, 'What's what?'

Lord, how do I approach the question?

How do i make known the secrets

because they are hard to bear?

They're always with and before me.

We share an unusual bond.

In jail, you were my maid,

my cleaner, and my mate.

In such a state calling through fear.

Near the end, not wanting to pretend.

Naked before you I stood.
Testament to how I live
became my home, and you
forgave me.
Each lie I told, I was shaken,
innocent to it and from it all.
Was ill, like a winter shade,
a shade that used to be my
crutch.

Precious Minds

Fine masses do exist
of a minor tone
and a tender kiss.
Mysteries open and unbound
succumb to a passing illusion,
fruition of an object
but objectively strong.
No wrong to be found
in our Saviour,
savouring   everlasting
manna,
heavenly styled and shaped.
A sudden loss of pain.
Rain to make flourish
pardoned our sins to nourish,
tenderly kissing, caressing
our precious minds.

Presence of Light

Crafting and searching for a
nurturing home.
Handiwork, leaving no stone
unturned,
Left in Rome, unbeknown to
us all,
cleft by the sight of little ones
in a state.
Gated, as stated, the love we
are all rated.
Sifting sandy, sensed sweet
shores purchased for us,
we must have time for the
sick and blind.

We follow the Father, who our
souls he is for.
The blood, sweat, and tears
through our years he wants.
Planted, planting a nation of
souls who do his work,
waiting for orders to start a
change in each other's spaces.
Grace, we are given enough
to erase the planet of sin and
dust.
Seek to find an answer for
farmers to parry the load,
a disowned love of which we
see too much of.

Frankly, it's best to clear out moth-eaten clothes

and bestow on us finely crafted clothes; our kin

with us, he is always our steps, the better bets, winners rest.

Don't detest one's freedom. Consider yourself blessed

because we have passed the test.

Right or wrong, we sing our songs and belong to one another.

Sisters and brothers, our bright sparks alight.

Consider yourselves to be fortunes to me.

Health is at work in you, so be healed, my friend.

But due to our work, you need the church and surplus rations.

Sometimes rational but thankful indeed.

Not one to read or bleed. Feed the needy with speedy action.

Millions add up to fractions, factional characters.

Measuring our atonement and enrolment in a service for good,

we understand but misunderstood due to listening to the underhanded

existing in our bubbles. Trouble here lets on the double.

Infallible and rational, our best friend is touchable.

Found out instead a man born and bred for a medal of metal.

Unsellable and undeniable to us; need to trust.

Murky months gone, the time had come to unwind the net,

betting on a sight of a trusty bird of flight.

Milestones of their own, far from homey homes.

Lives are made for good, I would say.

Members afraid to be lost.

The frosty, favouring, fallible foes, do choose their nooses.

Fatherhood, I understood the calling of the future histories

sent on a light of our mighty presences.

Universal stars, each one a gift from the Father of our souls.

Highs and lows, a fistful of foes brought to their knees.

Fees of our own families, setting us into fortune and colour,
found in the deep seas kept safe for our tomorrows.
Findings paint a pretty picture of our futures.

Presenting Favour

We shall try to be
as we see in Jesus—
calm, winding winds,
those fresh colours—
as we present to each other
the perfect gift in us.
You have restored me.
Your Word, your favour,
every good flavour
you have bestowed.
Gifts of lives filled.
A thousand hearts
daily shown to be
near my dear Father.

Protector

He dresses the flowers.
The fields are green,
the trees blossom,
and rivers run clean.
He feeds the possum,
hours apart,
specially.
His timing is perfect,
and so is he.
He rights our wrongs,
accepting us as children;
sings the bird's song,
mighty and true.
Such is the gift
he gives to you.

Pushing Forward

Insanely pretty,
her hair is curls of wool.
But nails sharp enough to deface.
Erase you from the earth,
turfed out into the cold,
for she said she can play.
But I pray she doesn't.

Bought at a high price
those men could not afford,
she is mine and not yours.
Off to the bank.
Oh, a change of heart
as she saw a man standing out.
His hair a wisp, the bark
loud and clear; she saw his
elegance.
The lowly but humble eyes of
a storm.
Formed a conversation
Through nothing at all.
The meeting lasted a few
seconds,
But long enough to spark a
change.
If I want him, he won't be
paying.
Playtime over. Over and out.

Your portion is there; don't
be late
as some are taken before they
rise.
Baffled, soldiers bruised,
soothed roots that drink
my sap.
Sap so sweet.
Better said than to deprive
of a man's will to survive.
Awesome wonder of the sight,
a quarantine with no
surprise.
Fed, watered, a place to stay.
My story would drift away,
but stationary we strongly
stand
in victory over all the sand.
Words we have are free to all.
Mountains crumble under
foot.

Quarantine

Blessed powers that be,
friendly giants from the sea.
It's a mystery for those strange
folk.
Poking and prodding for a
joke.
Speak up, speak up, my love.

Raised at Home

She saw him, oh, well
handled.
Raised to live a quiet life.
Found with a dismantled
smile.
Posted far away to war,

scars still raw and raised.
Took his chance of happiness,
And pulled it out of his hat.
Sam raised my son well,
Untarnished and well kept.
Brought out of despair.
The quiet lad bore the pain
a thousand raindrops cannot
contain.
Short of life but big of tender.
Slender age who does not
remember.
Far cry from the sad lad
he was.
Knew the tricks and now
secured,
fostering a homey home.
Kept with his wife, but not
his own.
Alone with his thoughts
about the lady in his youth
who took him for a ride.

Screened

Far from seen,
victory we feel.
Used to muddy boots,
flutes that call,

bringing triumph,
months of protest,
best-made friends,
ending current trends.
Surely I would not be
treated with disdain.
Hard-fought mind,
keeping pure and kind.
Calling birds,
screened for disease,
pleasing our fans.
Surely, all the days of life
will not be short.
Bought by precious blood,
minds understanding,
hearts pounding,
rooted and rounded.
Sound advice
coming back to life.

Sea of Change

How enchanted we are,
striking our posts,
entrenched with labours.
Will it end this way?
Is there no escape?
The search is over.

Can I come out to play?

Dusty like an unprotected,
unused lamp,

its dim light soon to be the
essence of colour.

Made dim by its neglect,

but colourfully select.

Rejected by its host.

Bright lights set in cavities.

Masterful brilliance

watered by the sea.

The waves and choppy
undercurrents

give a sense there is something
more.

This lighthouse is steady and
ready.

Its base is strong, and its face
is true.

Signed off on medical grounds,

stands like a proud man,

but someone who knows

growing for the prize ahead.

Well said wonders of the
seaman.

Stories of old never getting
tired of their power.

The grave is death, but our
lover is life.

Seas robbing our feet.

When we have no ship to
cling to,

we cling to our life-giver,

who sings into the wind

and blows it away.

There is a place where time
can erase,

struggling faces eroded.

Come to us, Jesus.

Bring us the life you want us
to live.

Forevermore we shall give of
ourselves.

Searching

We are due our rightful places

amongst the stars and the
gazing moon.

Time cannot erase a factual
promise.

Turning toward our beloved
Saviour,

our neighbour of love and
all truths

made to be honoured.

Youthful exposure came to
light.

When all we have is each
other,

it is enough to have and be.
Our collective beauty raised,
gazing upon the way we feel.
Come to life again, my shield.

Meals we share above and beyond.
Wheels in motion, strengthened.
Mentioned is the place we will be,
where love is the law,
and he who Christ loves
shall dwell in the place of the Most High,
turning the sky into light.
The grumbling, rumbling ground
and the fresh, free air of tomorrow,
tonight, and strengthened
until we have given it all.
No gift too small.
Let it all out and flow.
Then above the ground we know
what frequency behaves itself.
when all we have are noisy hustles.

A sight risen until sunrise is met
with a heavenly occurrence.

Second Watch

Counting those minutes,
cost to reason and bargain with.
Taking turns to look for spare time.
Spaces found to be complete.
Competing for a finished work,
Found and tried by Jesus.
Made to be solid and strong.
Lived through complete horror.
Finding his garments and walked,
stalked, and needed.
Fresh mind, body, and spirit.
A blessing we share and enjoy.
Furthermore, I should say
my wonderful lover and protector,
voice you want me to project.
Heavenward bound we are.
Bethlehem's bright star
Seen by watchers.

Shallow Tides

The lie of said goodbye
slowly fades to shallow tides.
Hallucinations grow to stir
unerring actions' advice.
Devising plans to rise
holy in his ways.
Sweet fruit to taste.
Let's not waste our gifts
of songs of prayer and praise.
Shallow graves
of the misbehaved,
don't run astray, aground.
The gentle sound of home,
whether London or Rome.
A two-way ticket; the boat,
don't miss it.

Shore Leave

Always be sure and believe
figments of mind retrieved.
Fragmented possibilities
hiding in the shade.
Bed made for a bride,
ready and undeprived.
Shore leave and wages
soon gone, but memories
lasting.
A bride of a sailor,
waiting in full hope
of a happy return,
murmuring sweet words.
A third of the heart
dedicated to a promise,
'Please be here soon.
Lift my soul and sail.'
Reunited in hope.
Ropes spared of work.

Signs

They ask for a sign
But listen not,
Rather, turn to crime
in some thick plot.
You need to know
there is little time
to share to care to love
to see; to believe
and be healed.
Sealed for eternity
Ones whom know you
faithfully release themselves

truly to you.
A harvest rite
of our fruitful endeavours.

Smile

The amazing act of giving
serving us with a smile.
Sensitivity occurring,
delights bountiful.
Across the border
the boundary, the fence.
Your smile breaks boundaries
and shatters the ice.
Deplores a natural sense
an arising, an awakening.
The sun bursts through
starry, starry nights
between me and you.
Pleasures in the sight
of our God.

Softly Spoken

She's quiet when she asks
for me,
a soft and quilted voice.

The moist sensation of my
choice.
Softly spoken reality kicks in.
Brethren, come forth and
sing.
Swingers in town don't bring
me down.
Fantasies of brotherhoods
made known.
Barely a breath, a whisper
delivering the greatest
message,
messages previously
unspoken.
Utterings of the broken heart.
The soul carries forth its
dignity.
Pretty and fast, mine meant
to last.
Came across a hushed
accusation
wanting a full conversion.
'Dearest queen, speak up.'
'Jesus, Jesus, Jesus, you there?'
'My dear, how do you know?'
'He is my breath, my boldness.'
'Who am I to judge my lover?
He is a part of me and sleeps
ahead,
ahead of my words, a shadow,
meadows of saintly interest.'

Sovereign

My Father, my teacher,
my protector, my healer,
I can see through the trees.
Have you seen me
down on my knees?
All of a sudden,
you take heed
of my love's lantern.
Hearing her precious words
spoken softly in love,
gently giving my heart's call
for my bride
never to fall.

Speak Up, Don't Fight

The night is over.
Feel what is there,
the ripples of the air.
Sip a little water.
Wait for a while.
He is always there,
waiting on your smile,
caring and sharing
your story.

The Lord knows your plight.
Don't fear.
No need to fight anymore.

Stand

You feel the plan.
Standing up under the pain,
times are tough
when you have nobody.
As for me, I can't quite grasp
the sensitivity of it all.
Stand for what you believe in.
Don't leave your life
in fortune tellers' hands.
He has a plan for your life
once you master and grasp the truth.
We feel you are there.
In your hand, a humble spirit.
Come over to me
and be where I am.
Settle on me.
Draught a plan where you search,
unrelenting until you have
all you need
and more

sorted in a timely fashion.
Came across a myth
that you will see through.

Starting Again

Disappointed but anointed,
subterranean plots appointed,
Tried and tested, what is
next?
The pipeline? Serving time?

The beginnings of a new story
The sanding down in progress
Processes old surpassed
Refusing to mask my smiles
It is just my style
To run the extra mile
Covered by the light
Sundried and drenched
His love in me secure

Pertaining to be what I am

State of mind

Finding our current state
elated with honour
come to my world

follow my lead
to bring forth and spread
the seeds of togetherness
humble ways to praise
at home to raise his spirit
without words we find
the kindness hidden inside
make my love your bride
don't push me aside
come for the ride
breathing our final breath
one after another
waiting for our spirit to
ascend
end of the days
come, fruit of our love
rise as a dove

Stating my case

For years I were encased
memory forgotten and erased
doctors saw no future
felt my time was up and
missed
stated my case at length
struggles past and gone
lives lived at an alarming
rate

dictating our ways we lived
together we discovered a plan,
a way to get out of their hands.
The hardy way, oh, I did pray,
suckling at the breast day
by day
until I was ready to chew
and eat.
Meetings flashed by without
a trace.
Not getting up today; took a
new way.
So pleased to be at home.
I roamed as if I wasn't my own.
Case solid and watertight,
took a ride home to live.
Sifting through notes and
papers,
giving me a chance to savour
what's mine.

Step 5

Our first step is to be gathered
on high.
Better start, and I know why.
Savouring fruits with much
supply.
Started my next step as he
wept.

The tears came down as we
went,
Spirit inside us, heaven sent.
Sweeter we are with our stars.
Step 3, we found our family,
taught to see what is meant
to be.
Sought heavenly gain is free.
Some far away believed
in me.
Tree to embark on a journey
sent as a gent on Calvary.
Step 4, we taught and tried.
With us in gain and want,
blessed we are to infiltrate.
My mate sat as we called for
that.
Passers-by set up the stage.
Fortuneless want comes to age.
Step 5, the best, as we ate
manna from heaven for we
wait,
assembled outside the rosy
gate.

Stories from long ago.

Where all we saw
were wind, rain, and snow.
The growth within us so far
on par with the bravery

we thought had gone.
The Son, our glory,
shared with a sip
a little wine and broke some bread.
Christ, the Godhead,
much said of the past.
Listen to what is raised,
like the sea-nurtured
brought up in the knowledge
of our saved souls.

Stormy Sunset

Surrounded by grace,
earthly passers-by,
ignoring the neglected,
were at the finish.
No turning back.
Sensory disturbances
on the right track.
No essentials do we lack.
Honest fathers
shaking us to begin
to repent of sin.
Missing teeth, broken
and again soaked.
No cough or choke.

Such and Such

You give and you take.
Maybe you will see another day.
Such and such said
I would be maimed.
How wrong they were.

Spiritually rooted and booted,
strong and brave,
to the core I see you.
Envisioned success,
saved to be a giver,
the strong, swirling tides
of a river to a blind man
scarcely making a move,
stunned by the journey
and its simplicity,
he let go.

Falling and tumbling,
steel will and strong longing
for his Saviour
to become his
fortune favours us.
We just need to trust.

Sundays

Sundried Saturday nights,
polite regards for a good night,
we are the church,
where we seek God.
Modern ways gone out today.
Maybe we feel connected.
Success comes easily free,
the meal that keeps us going.
We chose the right path.
Mothers, fathers, sisters, brothers,
Join in hands with one another.
We talk of the ways of Christ.
Waysoftheworlddisconnected.
We are sent to share and show
what God has done for us both.
Enough to be with him on the path.
We worship you for all you are,
set on high, and brought us home.
Tonight is the night for rest
because we need it for tomorrow.
Set on high, and brought us home,
bellowing all the way,
like the wind taking us to Paradise,
to the Lord, who is my home.
In his heart, we are safe.

Sunny skies

The whit of one explores chaste did he know?
But overthrown due to mass departures,
then unbeknown until after, our sainted martyr didn't see the truth.
Counted each and every lover till our manhood came.
The saving of our souls came at a price—bloodshed.
Baffled brains could not maintain their sorrow.
They have today, but what of tomorrow?

Oh, they did borrow to excess.
Days came and went like a seasonal-dressed empire.
Plans they had and came to naught,
deciding to buy what was already bought.

Our teacher and friend never to see us fail without reproof.

Soothing our souls to battle on, win the good fight,

with all your love strapped, striped, and light to night.

Our time will come when enough is enough.

Our fountain crashing, flowing, and slipping to us

maintains to overthrow what was never theirs.

Fractures never a match for the bold and brave,

saved and not mislaid but spread across this globe.

Soapy seas seeded with my wife untouched

for the sweat of my brow contained until bestowed.

For the morn is near, closer than ever before.

Stars leapt on the sight of our sparkling eyes

as our kindly surprise opened the skies.

Glory in the highest defies reasoning, belief.

Here to achieve our salvation of all time.

Stripped, mapping out our saving plans; just understand

I died for you, so you don't need to be

Fed, nurtured, watered, born out of love.

Seeking our smiling faces always,

we live in a daze, wondering if we can run the race.

Morals alive for I am yours, and you are mine.

Everyday signs keeping you alive.

Sweeping Thoughts

She lies low,
Hoping for her debutant to go,
knowing who he was and is
petrified of letting her know
abstract stories of loss and gain.

Does anyone know her pain?
Refraining from entertaining,
where is her home?
Letting a mere obligation
moving from raised herds,
settling down for a moment,

catching escaping breath.
Paused, confused.
Bruised by sweeping thoughts,
rushing by lame incoherency,
brought out to find
she left someone behind,
Blinded by the loss.
Glossy covers bossing attire.
Must be my love, my fire.
Hidden desire
creeping up on her.

Swimming the Tide

Praise goes heavenward in grace.
No time to waste these days.
We swim with the tide and ride,
fought to be here tooth and nail.
Facing the soul,
the tides, the rides
plucked up the courage to think.
Thoughts can make a home in our heads
more precious than mothers' money.

What are the times and days
when we are fresh and others age?
Plastic coffins broken free
past the tired and blameless,
fortuneless and mightily blessed.
Do change; wear a dress.
Lord, I need to laugh and love.
To desire to live not in a shift.
Many roads to our love sought.
The one I find is the kindest.
The treasure vault of your heart opens.

Tailored to suit

My dear, we fit
like a well-tailored suit.
Dressed to impress
all the guys pursue.
From the hat to the shoe,
no match for any of you.
Count the numbers
far and wide.
We fit, my love,
to sit and to take this ride.
My match, my fire,
my head, and heart's desire.

Taken for a Ride

She falls for the tall ones.

Oh, how she rose.

Felt a little elated,

the past still a thorn in her side.

Taken for a ride many times,

but not anymore.

Bitten lip and a little sore,

don't wanna dance no more.

Seeking comfort and peace,

she came to a standstill.

Can't quit now, nearly there.

Rose, born of fair circumstance,

bereft of clothes.

But still a sense of decency,

relaxed her pose and with raised nose,

solemnly declares, 'No more!

No more drinking, eating, chewing.

I'm all chewed up.

Don't know what I am doing.'

Then he stood, chest and all,

six foot two with a staggering smile.

'Here is one who

I can bear his child.'

Talk

We belong to love and were near,

staring at each other in no fear.

Dizzy, but holding it together.

Sever contacts if you feel to

bring him to me, with me

sing a long song sincerely.

Tears streaming from battery;

senses overloading from flattery.

What really matters to me?

If we talk, we share what's there,

combining truths and seeking out friends.

No doubt in our minds floating.

Fruitfully arisen, a toast to you.

Thoughtfully, we see a picture.

Nurture our family.

Missed loved one in tandem.

Randomly searching for fruit,

The fruit we have tasted,

manna so sweet, and long

searched for you the best.

Testing a line, food so divine.

Take me aside and say what's what.

It's a plot we follow.

Love we seek to remove sorrow.

Borrow my pen to talk again.

Seek what's lost that is in the wind.

Free our tongues to belong.

A richer taste, a sweeter song.

The Blood

The giving life blood
pressures inside our hearts.

An internal storm,
chopping, changing, waiting.

Rest coming soon, he prays.

A small whisper he hears.

The heir of sailors,
a plentiful harvest to enjoy.

The fish came home.

But another wait,
a wait too long for many.

A semblance of faithful,
forced to eat at the table.

But it's our blood that fills us.

The Depths

For some time I thought about
the rawness of it all.

Flowers and rainfall,
rivers bursting their banks,
searching and feeling our ways.

Becoming a true and certain man.

Buried
beyond reason for a final dance.

Essence of our beings
released to live our ways.

Certain to find our own ways.

Seeking a journey past today.

Praying because we all need to say

how our days are numbered.

Keeping in all certainty

due to the ways we sing.

Following in awe, coming clean.

Tall, wide, and broad.

Hired guns fall aside.

The bells chime.

Trial and tribulations,
a morrow of transformation
for every heart and every
nation.
A hearty taught lesson
on the depths that went forth
into praise of our souls,
ignited first and seen by all.

The Destination

Oh, hello my bonnie
Englishman.
How did your journey bring
you here?
Did you find rest and sleep
with the bandwagon rolling?
Join us, and be merrily
accepted.
Invited you are. A
sentimentally bizarre
family with our family
begins.
Become a Scotsman and live.
Our lives are simple and fair.
We do declare our love freely,
washing us clean, briefly
speaking,
with happy and helpful
spirits.

Invited we are; fall we don't.
Feathered hats and fancy
skins.
Destined for our saintly
pilgrimage,
walking, talking, brought
before our King.
Our King rules with love and
insight;
follows the path of
righteousness.
Finely dressed in feathers
and love.
Our loving King, full of grace.
Bend me, Lord, so I can taste
your flavour and spirit.

The Figure

Many sensed a flutter,
a heart's figurine
taken a man's flesh.
Dig deeper and find
the treasure inside.
Our minds are fresh.
I figured this one out,
moving lips, a dismount.
This figure hidden
but cannot hide.

Must be forgiven a many
life found in memory.
Picturesque bodies
embodied with light,
thus shadow's polite cause
hidden, bought, treasured.
Our lives in Christ's hands.

The Journey

It is a certainty we grow older.
Walking shoulder to shoulder
with reverence to bolder
journeys.
Fanciful that we are doing
our parts,
a start beyond what is
perceived.
Receipt of a gift faintly
estimated.
Jolted while I think.
Sinking not an option or
course.
Bring me my parrot for
guidance,
happily held in residence by
some.
Where are we going? What
about food?

Brewing up a storm in the
kitchen,
followed by a wave of taste
buds forming in the belly.
Fortune awaits with mystery.
What about history forgotten?
Tuning into the wireless
muttering,
making us aware of trouble.
An answer sounds within,
chattering examples.
A brief, brief moment of
truth.

The Often Mocked

The offence was cruel.
Unjustification, hence the
sentence.
A spirit within,
the plan born formed a thorn
in his side; taken for a ride.
All inside from the lies of
liars,
mocked and burdened.
Death awaiting.
Concentrated evils prying,
waiting
for a crack in Christ not
found.

Bound in chains but unafraid,
the task surrounding made
a sense of loss, a grenade.
Thousands gave cost to the lost,
while millions called in sick.
Levels of urgency stuck, ran amuck.
A stocked lake, workers few,
bringing our food to you.

Your Son's Palette

The wash, cleansing impurity.
His son's painted face
offers a taste of freedom.
His role in his story
needs a brighter, glowing face.
Natural taste and tendencies,
tenderness in his mirror.
Collapsed without cause.
Hastily climbs the ranks.
Disregards himself but resists
forces that be in nature.
Changed men to deface the face.

The son who began to dig
a life has become so big.
Back to the son's palette.

Your Palette

You smudged me by the sea
with personality finding company.
The brush blushed in art
to the corner of her brow
brought back to life somehow.
The sand the palette
drew, washed, rebuilt,
smudged, delved, dug, scraped.
Overdone and causing a stir,
using me as bait.
Not now' it's half past
half a palette, half a girl.
That colour for a lady?
Don't cast your pearls to swine.
Find yourself in colour.
Live and love like no other.
Do us proud: Be life, be loud.

(All poems mastered, arranged, and deployed by Timothy Green.)

The Place, the Time

Our place is here.
Our time is now.
We will find our ways.
Faces portraying our story,
grasping and clasping
onto a hope we all have.
Homeward bound,
but not bound by laws.
We, his children,
must force a change.
Not change-givers
but storytellers.

The sail, the Face

Yonder, further into the fond, waves
grasped the clean sheets; along it carried.
Yardarms swung freely to the sound of the wind,
bringing a slight ease found in the doubting eye.

Stormy seas thrust ease of struggle and sight.
My love, you know the silent night so well.

Facing the sail with strong undeterred hope,
sloped forth the deep feeling of a broken man.
Cuts were deep numb and raw,
sun-dried, giving of light and sight.
Were the friends of the content kite
free, bright, and following?

The Start of My Heart

Bellowing on the surface
made me a little nervous.
Surplus to requirements,
sentimental start and finish.
My heart starts again.
My Saviour, who died,
took my name and made it strong.
You belong to me, my love.
It's enough to make me weep.
Another week in secrecy.

Another day of praise and wage.

Coming of age today, and always

it's ticking; my heart is ready, ready to blow and burst.

Ready to follow, to grow.

Patched up every day.

A real certainty nervously awaits.

Follow and clean, clean and new.

You are mine, and I am yours, brought together again.

The summit

Fair play, we will meet someday.

Praise his name in the heavens.

Praise his name on all the earth.

The summit is near and calling,

panning out blessings all morning.

No yawning of the morning.

Sitting before the sea breeze,

humbling myself and on my knees.

In the distance, the horizon.

Fed and watered, we cool down.

Total peace we send to earth.

Nothing less than the best is mine.

Children and the young, see certainly you are blessed your whole life.

Princely sums amounting to dust.

All the time I wish I had left, gone over to your room.

We have a birthed offspring.

For hours we learn to sing.

Summit closes.

So far, we are who we are.

The swan

She enters the stage—

lakes suit her—

drenched in a fine garment.

Who told her to swim?

No one but I.

Bought at a happy place.

The rates were not hers.

Finally, it clicks.

Penny drops, but not hers.
Served at the perfect time.
Cool as ice, she points northward.
Homeward.
Sentimentalities are an occurrence
best suited to her own.
The prize, a splendid hello.
Worth the wait is she.
Waiting for her suitor.
Suitable to the highest order.
Monthly, she waits for better.
When it's right in her breath,
leaving without a word, a glimmer.
Such a fine swimmer.
Another night alone.
She sewed her own suit.
Laced and bound,
chicks in pursuit,
bound in their taste.
Tracks erased.

The Tin Man

Known for his humble shoes,
his beaten mind,
the bruise unseen or heard,
choosing not to share his purse.

The tin man sneered as he ran,
not one to follow the crowd.
Mistaken for a coward,
took his shoes, and they were amused.
He had the last laugh.

He focused on his mind.
Information, truth he does find.
They thought they knew it all,
but they were blind.
Taking to the sea, the wind in his sail,
no need for an address; no way to get mail.

'Aye-aye, Captain,' he laughed.
'Our paths meet again, young King.'
Not through necessity or distress,
but a true longing for his Creator.
The laughter, tears, bloodshed, scars—
all for love.

Sailing towards the east, succumbed to a passing feast.

'At ease, sir'; he threw his boots, beret, pass.

'A new life for me?' he asked.

The gentle son waking his days,

leading his path to the ends of the waves.

'Struggle over my king, my being.'

Searched high and low for somewhere to go.

But in his heart, needing none.

Bricks don't make a place, nor space a rest.

The Winning Ticket

So much to say, so little to do.

New grass and brewed like it was meant to.

Animals running,

chewing on whatever is free.

Take me not too far east,

where windmills break into song.

It is where I wish I could be.

My winning ticket not given away.

Shared if you would, kind sir?

It was meant for me from my father.

Gifts are for the life-giver

Mountain of costs given as a gift.

It is mine and meant for me.

Contrast in statements,

Made in patience.

Payments due as the reality subdues.

Come over and sing with me.

Our thoughts are our guide.

Miles high above the clouds,

surrounded by love,

chased through the air,

like a kite gasping for breath.

Take me up.

Never let me go.

I am winning and free.

Don't disown me as the folks have

because I would surely be in waiting.

I have more time,

and I am not wasting it.

This Feeling Is for You

My dear, how do you feel
when you have a real choice?
Boisterous boys making noise.
Clarinet blown through
charmingly
disarmed, dismantled,
no more or less to handled.
Fanciful fluttering pages
spoke of our Lord through the
ages.
No ageing for us in Christ.
Mere time cannot decline us
from into his trusting arms
we are handled.
Fanatics call for a battle.
Not on my watch, we settle
down.
Feelings of our lovers' touch.
Unbroken, the skin loved so
much.
Such a waste to life in haste,
said to taste, feel
a better way to be.

Those Delicate Two

The pause of the shores
rattled beneath delicately.
Oh, the delicate but strong
fawn beneath the ocean.
Oceans of laughter hails
The King is born.
Not out of wedlock.
Not from the dust,
the dusty settlement
of a loud, booming cloud.
Centred among the righteous,
popped pill of ease.
Trees falling beneath
a somewhat happy sky.
Laughter of the lark.
Out until dark then home.
A masculine aroma.
The carried burden lifted,
a gift for the gifted.

The Trumpeting sound

If thy manor hath found
abiding in love,
I am a blessed man indeed.

If thy gave a hundred,
then my thousand aside
tried and tested valour.
If you found manna tasted
by kings and queens
and satisfied our friends,
our fathers take us home
if you bear my harvest.
Shared to all the call,
the trumpeting sound
bringing Christ home,
where the heart is born
and the soul is calm.

Time We Have

Little hours to spend
as we wish with hope.
Better and kinder tomorrows.
We taste of the vine,
and it tastes our hearts,
needing and thriving
the contact we have.
Souls we hold and reflect,
his glory needing to bare.
Born from a lover's kiss,
we enter freedom.
Seldom do we ask of the task

required to reap and sow.
Favourite plans born of
seclusion in peace.
Fond of the memories
and future place.

Times of Change

Time is not a commodity
underlining   positive
change.
No change, but paid in full.
Surrender of the youth.
Sound advice is the truth—
my truth, our truths.
These are strange times
and even stranger people,
all needing a Saviour.
Plenty of him to go around.
No select pardons,
all who love our Lord
and keep in the faith.
He is our selected Father
mother, sister, brother.

Times to Be Held

Foreseen truths on hold.
Forlorn 'twas for an adult.
Searching journeys
but found this prayer.
'Twas night, Lord.
Polite was his giving.
I found giving a joy
found in a fountain.
Treasures misspent,
sent he was from sight.
Forbidden swords
attack none, and lay waste.
Times to be held,
felt at peace.
Found my treasure.

To Give

All sorts; outside and inside
brought to us a certain pride.
Elegance of a well-said
thanks.
Dancing around tables
from an English influence
to an earthly pretence.
Forged in victory and incense,
we are able to share and give.
Sought out the real to sift.
Give we ought how to live.
That way we want to believe,
to retrieve the hope to share.
Bearing the weight,
drying our eyes to nurture.
Beginnings of good character
tempered   at   high
temperature.
We come home for love.
What did we find but the
blinded—
blinded to pain, fear,
entrapment.
Traps set but skillfully miss
a dancing pair getting there,
bearing to be noticed on high.
Went out under good supply.
Children's tears of happiness,
knowing we care.
Blessed in giving.

To Reason With

Oh, my dear reason,
how do I satisfy your need?
I feed you daily,
but you respond not.

I tithe you, I save you,
but you give of yourself rarely.
Feeding on your words,
every mere morsel you give,
a sprinkly sprinkling,
dusty and dry.
But of you I can say, 'Well,
the depths of wisdom
of those mere morsels
are short and sweet, and your
words
taste them and see.

Today

Exhilarating, freshly cut
fields
built on tomorrow's plans,
taught to reply to unidentified
minds fed with dreams untold.
Boldness unearthed and
ready.
Steady the ship's hull so
heavy.
Chased from the chase and
brought home,
deservedly happy in the
zone.
Memories await a tender kiss,

missed and missing a thought.
Dreams seeking a subtle
reality,
sought after love and joy.
Undertaking a new song
belonging to the heavenly
realm.
Earth made rule seldom felt.
Tried and tested, all invested
in the name on high.
We multiply our thoughts
and reason
in the right seasonal ways.
A dollar a night, a pound
a day.
The waves pounding the
shore,
seen, washed, and dried.
Today and always, plenty of
supply.

Touched

Here I find you now.
You were broken;
now you are alive.
Somehow, we see your heart,
your truth that starts you up.
Like a handle that has been
pulled

yanked into reality, readily awakened

against the pliant world,

where it is normal to hurt.

Normal to wait and to sometimes wail.

Weeping as our friends depart.

The touch you seek is far from home,

Far from the riots and from time.

It's almost certain to cause a rift,

the way we are in regards to the world.

Certainty with authentic voice,

touching things we shouldn't,

electric shivers and the rush

caught up together, all from fun.

But is it real?

Is it right?

Further calling from our Father.

The high place placed

on a step where we are not neglected.

Special mentions

for all who want out.

Further, we try to find out

the realities we speak of,

shown ways to be held on high.

It's our family who gifts us,

sifting and shaking the maze of life.

Transformation

By his standard we rise.

By our standards we drag.

With colour he sets us apart.

Coming in from the cold,

we lay and sing.

He pulls and draws us up.

Silence we make,

but he is as loud as rain

and dry like a cloudless sky.

But it is his power that can change.

The transformation that builds

caresses our fields for food,

life-giving food.

Taught to love and bear,

sought after since time began,

lives now with his presence.
His light that shines forth we follow,
bringing good news
for the needy we make well.
Riches follow us all the days.
Our lives are never the same.
Always before and behind and with us.

Travelling Pair

Fist fight over.
Ran off to clothe her nakedness.
Tissues sodden,
revealing her openness.
Downtrodden and made to fear.
Gotta get out of here.
Amassed a wealth of scars.
Brutality finished.
The car, her way out.
Slipping away.
A minute a day, portraying
bravery written all over her.
Guarding her getaway.
Went without a tear.
Near to death,

escaping with her heart intact.
Soul bearing the hurt.
Children never deserted.
Blamed for being alive.
It's over now.
Take a bow for her.

Treasure

My treasure, I found your love.
I gathered into my bosom
and kept it all inside.
But that's not its place.
Time and space cannot erase
the deep longings for her.
Our treasures are the same.
Don't bottle it up;
do not sell it for a reward.
Keep it safe from the sword.
Share our deep longing
for a place we can call home.
To roam naked
under the starry days,
live not in a blind haze,
that maze leads to an exit.

Unity

My lady and I,
what a lovely surprise.
No disguise.
When I look in your eyes,
my girl I found.
A love so free,
unbound but together.
Feathers of protection
to gain a reaction.
Provocation and action
solved the puzzle.
A little lift
comforting.

Waiting for a Miracle

What were you taught
when ready for time to pass?
Class dismissed.
Diminished responsibility,
ability to present a master
plastered in hope and agility,
frailty withdrawn from
studies,
thought to be better than
most?

Post-laughter revenge
wanted,
sorted, and salt in the wound.
Blazed above the bar,
racing for the privileged,
steering into the wind.
Kin in doubt about their
safety
suddenly felt an arm of
protection
pushing toward the shore.
Before we knew it,
we were home and dry.
Abundance of grace and
protection.
Angels felt a direction
and a longing for peace and
life.

Waiting

For a little while,
caught undressed walking in
my dreams.
They were trodden but still
recognizable.
Beyond the surrounding
chaos,
he managed to learn and
ponder.

Sat in his seat, a chair of all time,

amassing a wealthy boon of lives,

living many.

Sent to bring hope and prosperity,

but mainly love and joy.

Took his life and washed clean his shirt.

Took it to many places.

Now it is settled on an island.

To the top, he pushes steadily on.

Goal in sight, record timing.

So close, and then the race is called off.

No losers counted,

participants rewarded.

Floored by the weight of expectation,

still held in high regard and esteem,

friends of England.

Warm

My sweet, you give to me

seeds I need to breathe upon.

Attention you give,

equipped to handle my whims.

Every day is another victory.

Seeking my smile earnestly,

my sweet, you are to me

the fresh air

and spring leaves.

High seas filled with beauty,

you are my bounty.

A week-old decade.

The forged works

shaped with love and care.

We Are sailing

Never failing for our successes,

meat to the bone and in dresses,

delivers our timing by the bell.

The whistle sounding at pitch.

Awake at five, not much to do.

Watching those waves and skies.

Not alone for my Lord is with me.

Gazing eyes look back to the sea.

See, my little friend,
an heir to the throne.
Finding a game to rest my own.
Calling to me, the wind in
shapes.
No mishaps fallen onto my
name.
Here we go, sailing away
into the romance of a wind-
made harp.
Suddenly, my heart melts.
We are sailing in our dreams.
Fortified protection,
reams of plaster
bring me joy, everlasting
laughter.
The anchor is drawn up.
Sailing here on after.

We Can say

Without the tongue,
we can spread messages.
Without the pen,
but we cannot live
until we know Christ.
We have tears
of a number of years,
but a moment's silence

can break the lock.
Passed to share,
words of the tongue.
Too young to know.

We Found You

You were tired and lonely,
waiting for your world to
happen.
When once you were called
out of a trap,
what happened?
Is it called entrapment?
Sought help and a beginning,
a new day and a break
from someone else's mistake.
Take me away to another
world.
Turns in time with my
heartbeat.
Take for yourself a comfy seat,
and you shall be shown
all you have been grown to
understand,
a wondering hand,
a Father's plan just for you,
perpetually understood and
remembered.

We Walk, We Talk

This timely equation in our heads,

turning ourselves towards our beds.

Luxury murmurs inside the mind.

Kindness prevails every time, from comical to the sublime.

Sought after rocks inside the mine.

When we walk, we talk in stride.

Bountiful hearts met inside.

Let's take a ride somewhere nice.

Have home time and a Brie.

Miming and mining have their places,

searching, motioning to their mates.

State of these times fortuneless.

Dressed to the nines but unimpressed.

Sad state when we digress

back to reality; hearts were a mess.

Distress taught me to fear.

Love drew me back again

into my Father's heart,

where to start and finish my work.

Deservedly so.

Stowing away memories to display.

We prayed.

There is something real about you.

We seek the truth of you,

walking in your way,

talking as if it's your last day.

What Is the End?

How do we fathom

simplicity in its deepest form?

When will we see heaven,

Father in all his glory,

end to the plight or story?

The story continues.

Fighting for breath

on this earth of striving,

some surviving but not living.

We believe what is true.

The sails of the saints

painting a perfect picture

away from sinister plots.
Dotting around and impartial
marching on in grace.

What We Found

Following a discussion, we
agreed
to follow our hearts
and not our greedy elements.
Water heating our bones,
somewhat prone to the cold,
sentiments are stirring us.
Action is waiting for a start.
Parting ways but still drawn.
The battle is there
to be fought and won.
Back to where we started,
the church has its land.
We would look after it,
looking out for lambs and
wolves.
For those cruel enough to kill
and strip.
Breaking bones for fun.
But not on my watch.
So I looked, poised, ready.
From my position, I lay in
wait.

Wolves were near,
trying to eat from my plate.
'Not on my watch,' I shouted.
Thinking twice, they were
not up to the fight.

Why We Live

It is adjacent and true.
Fond brilliances anew.
Forever our days.
Our Father we praise.
Why we live
past end of days,
not fazed or dazed.
Paths we all need
to follow while we plan it.
Growth of our due reason.
Enough of all frozen food.
The fresh honeydew
smooths the heart
and calms the soul,
raising our inner spirits
enough to learn because
these times are precious.
Inner measures so
filling to my mind.

Wishing Well

Are you my well, dear, to sip from?

Much more than a sip, rather a dip.

Sensing a rather forward maid,

when is it set for? What times?

Not wishing to undermine your elegance,

pretence not the way to praise.

Passers-by not defacing but erasing.

You are the well of my youth,

over the years unaged,

But for you, my darling, I would share.

Scarcely aware of the time,

she catches a hint of taste

the vine makes when it shows itself,

not wanting to be left there, dying.

Plastered on all walls, shaking,

my well-mined well trivial.

Someone seeking a miracle

needed a response for responsibility.

Under the tree we felt our vows.

Grows and groans beyond your own,

sown in circles by my face,

brought the maid to wander in want.

Wells wished for back in the garden.

Words

On your throne, Lord,

you have many shapes.

On your throne, Lord,

we know who you are.

On your throne, Lord,

a peacefully nested heart.

On your throne, Lord,

were never second best.

We know you are real.

We believe you are real.

Someone so surreal,

appealing for us to know you,

the love you are.

We are sealed by our holy spirit,

and we use our lives

serving you, Lord, with a smile.

Pining for you and your words,

slowly showing us we are of good use.

Amazingly so, we are running through

our blood, our minds, our souls, our cries.

Not sitting down, we need to unite.

Brought us to a preciously healthy state of mind.

Behold the writing song to write.

Fortune, jewels, grand designs come to naught if you are not there.

Willing to serve you, so deserve to be born again and

my birth such an honour of which can we ponder?

Young and Brave

Bring me all the young and the brave

searching for answers,

behaving for success,

planting our futures

sown flawlessly.

Partake of our customs,

the bread the body,

life-giving blood.

Drink, eat, be merry.

Be part of our growing community.

Songs from an angel

worthy of honour and praise.

Words can say so much

in so few words,

surfacing hidden issues

rescued from oblivion.

My task to ride to the end,

spreading the Word

of the lover inside,

our Jesus, our Lord.

Your Name

Just put it here.

No pressure, my dear.

You catch your breath,

never lagging.

backpacking the world,

searching for that place

where there is no time or space.

Memories erased,

but your name stands known.

Growing or groaning,

slowly towing our ship

to the road it goes

until blackout.

We just don't see

what our future has been made to be,

for us we share

the same name as our Maker.

Not shaking in fear,

to the show, my dear.

Fleeting notions of grandeur,

it's all in a name.

From me to you,

Passed down the family jewels.

Tools used

taught me well.

Yours sincerely

You can go far with whom you are.

As you go through life wondering,

pondering, seeking our stars,

Jesus is our star, never far away.

He brought us home; we were going astray.

Traits await a pleasant picture.

Not just one,

but a taste of mixture.

Wherever you are, call

whenever you can from on high.

Trying to be patient,

look at the sky.

Father, we seek out the meek.

His unique creation gets a mention.

Delegating and problem-solving,

half the matter, half the size.

Brought to you with a smile,

dodging the missiles.

Yours sincerely nearly early.

The tears are in me for a cry.

Found a place where you can dry.

Signs, sighs, and shapes

brought to paste and please.

On our knees, waiting for peace.

Unease fading beyond the seas.

We half believe the story.
Bounty in glory our story.

Youthful Expression

We delight in expression.
The tongue, the eye
satisfy me greatly.
The joy, the energy
facing north,
childish diplomacy.
Not so subtle hints
of favours.
Less than a childish man,
a child of the inner parts,
sobbing   for   systematic
departures.
breathing the fresh air,
young martyrs made.
A look inside,
our bodies barely worn.

At the seams

You are here.
That's good enough.
Shed me a tear
made of strong stuff.

Storming off in a huff,
the smoke-filled room
rises until
it has nowhere else to go
but out the window.

Searching for a little place
to hide and supply,
in the shade
where there is cover.
Outnumbered   and
outgunned,
they shed their habits.
Rising costs of inflation,
infatuation, trial and error
float away
as the room feels
a heavy lift.

At the seams we are strong
men of the cloth
and of the belt buckle
of truth.
Grounded in faith,
holding fast until that day
the return of the King,
bringing supply and power.
Crashing and casting aside
the vile,

the unbelieving,
rejecting our Lord,
bringer of peace and justice.

Be still

I am with you always.
Not just a passer-by
searching your face.
I see my joy.
Curtain torn and certain.
Raise your voice and say
to me, 'I am your way.'
Caught in the middle,
praying masterfully
with my story told.
Not getting ill
or getting old.
Shoulder to shoulder,
I carry you there.
Your body and glaring eyes
raise a stare of hurt,
past hurts.
Blurting out words
better left unsaid.
But they are mine,
and I choose to say them,
revealing my destiny

unfolding unto me.
Concern left my heart,
and now I am happy for you.
Journey you came from,
where are you now?
Showered in colour,
you are my child,
and I care for you.

Becoming (Version 1)

Audaciously, I ask thee,
'How do you work your
chivalry,
your brave and courageous
spirit,
daring and gallant fortitude.'

Comeandgivemedeliverance,
freedom to do and speak what
is right.
A fearless, hardy heart,
where nerves are taken away
and put somewhere else.

May I gab without making
sense?
Would I want to?
Shying away from all
pretence,

the wire lengthens where discourse goes.
Stretch out your hand and be healed,
sealed with my, our Spirit.
Speak with me, and I will show you
planetary shift evolving for and with you.

The pleasure that we dwell in
rubs me until I feel my lengthened days.
We praise our Father.
The true author of creation
would like a mention,
though painted and echoing walls,
the sky and the floor,

keep me intact.
Reacting to my every move,
undiluted fantasy
carry me home.

Bilingual

I didn't choose my language.
And I never chose my mother.
Undercover and uncovered,

left in spite of my efforts.
Best keep it at home,
where I roam.
And it is my decision
to live this way
and with who I choose to stay.
Praying for someone beautiful,
a doting mother wed undercover,
sent like no other.
And my brother to tidy me up,
to take away the lonesome feelings.
My Father knows it all,
and he shares with me
his plans and my pleas
for readiness.
Ready to live my life
pleasing to my Father.
Rather be here than out there.
So come on, and live a little.
You are young but a little brittle.
Battleships waging wars,
but it has been done before.
Brothers and sisters united
around the world, we press for peace,
for truth and justice.

Whatever language you speak,
seek first the Lord,
his meekness and softness.

By the Hill

Instilling me with a sense of purpose,
a little nervous and afraid
of the words that cower inside my mind.
You know, the ones that tower in the innermost.

But I have my Jesus, and he keeps me new.
Fresh as a daisy, the dew is due.
Tenderly, he sees the cold, hard matter.
My platter yields to you.
Certain of certain truths enfolds me.
Talk to me; I know you are there,
waiting on some time to bare your thoughts.
My thoughts are in you and with you.
Tasting those bleeding hearts,

I wish to make them beat.
Seated on high, where all good you see,
turning your face from sin,
but not the sinner.
By the hill you were young and free.
I sensed your purpose deep inside me.
Believe and receive, my sweetheart.
Turning to you, we never part.

Such a state, but now treated as first rate.
Call on me, and I shall be a mate
beyond all the stares.
Who is he, and why is he there?

Casting a Care

My love, I find you there,
waiting and hesitating.
Casting my cares on your back.
Supplicating and mesmerizing,
never at all in lack.

Casting my worries on you,
my yoke is light.
Learn from me, and you will find
kindly natured figures
now no longer blind.
Factually righteous,
courteous, and wise,
this prize is ours.
Come to me,
and stay true to me.
Covered and finely tuned,
not at all subdued
because, Lord, you give me
the food I need
for this journey.
Thank you, Father,
for keeping me perky,
and my plans for us.
You shall become
a rock of my place,
built with you in mind.
I search and see you.
You cannot hide.
Nurturing your calm mind,
beginning to feel and believe.
Taught you well.
Seeing my seed grow.

A wonderful man, you will know
my wisdom and strength
I bestow on you, my child,
my friend.

Chase It Away

It is courtesy to say
when you need to leave
and why.
In the course I take,
wondering eyes meet,
but they quickly hide themselves,
scared of intimacy.
Where it is likely to hurt
blurting out promises,
regrets beyond our minds.
Kindly share my load,
and I shall carry
what I am able to,
but you know that anyway.
Swaying trees in the midst,
I would climb them if I could.
Not to be misunderstood.
The wooden pieces of our hearts,
deserted of varnish,

ruffled and scuffed.
But with a little love
just as new, and better.
These letters I give
have a place of honour
in our hearts.
No waste there.
No departures and no scarring.
All new inside.
Now to either bride or hide,
and it is my choice.
I have the ability
to make my voice heard.

Chasing the Dream

'My team,' I call my friends,
family, and fun.
Oh, we never end.
Contact retracts at times,
but back soon.
Summary of the dream
basically sat.
Serenity comes
and floats my boat.
Choking underneath the oak
trees that formed matter.
Keep dreaming

of a platter of dreams,
seemingly real and surreal.
My meal is ready,
cooked steadily.
Merry is my hook.
Turning to you,
my brew is wild.
Children smiling
Whilst I'm in hiding.
Chiding my food,
riding that taste,
my hunger erased.
Chasing your mind,
you are the loving kind.

Choose with Me

With you, it's all so new,
craftily judged to be true.
For wealth of men can change,
given the odds
for a staged performance.
But it's not your way.
You have it,
and I pray you stay.
Use and care wisely
as the added tools
pass their case

inspection, awaiting
for my puzzle to be made
clear from misjudgements.
Stacked are the odds
mentioning the calls.
Doves of the north
calling sparrows of the south.
Not placing any doubts
on this time with us.
With you I can be clear.
Not wanting a case to make,
it's already here.
Wise men do say
to clear your mind,
removing fear from you.
Choose with me
the love of my dreams.
Sisters are calling
to bring reams of film.
Your show,
and you are the star.

Come Home

Coming with you,
this wondrous task,
somethinggreatishappening.
I sharpen my allure.

Set before me a shore,
stirring up waves of emotion.
Oceanic praise is for you.
Your nectar blows in the
wind.
Forgiveness of sins,
my friend, starts to begin
searching for a place
to bring you in from the cold.
My joy I give you,
sent with love.
Messenger from above,
cover these issues.
Out of tissues;
I don't need them anymore.
Store, for the time is right
to give us what you have.
Sending your spirit
a wonderful treat.
Depleting armies
looks to be his war.
comrades watching
as those armies will fall,
stalling and floundering.
Us, as his anointed ones,
tough but soft.
It is a great mix.

Delight in My servant

Holding all the cards,
substantially truthful,
playing fairly,
fun to be had.
Bleed me dry of inadequacy.
Empty me of all pride.
Cast my illness aside.
Throw away my doubts.
Knead me into shape.
Bend me with your nape.
Roll me without tolls.
Crush my insanity.
Brush away my riches;
they are as dust to you.

These days are long,
and the fight is on.
Where the strong
are as bendable as metal
under heat,
we decide to feature
our lovers' kindness.
Keep together my plan,
the plan for humanity—
all of humanity.

Selfless acts of kindness
never ceasing.

Believe me,
he is real,
more real than any rock
that took a good climb,
tall and vast,
climbing upwards
to the heavens.
We can't keep up
by our own powers.
His faith shared
brings us closer
than ever before.

Dewsbury

Having seen you,
touched you
with my fingers,
I can say
that you are there,
waiting for us.
Believing in you
could be our tickets
to somewhere beautiful.

Missionaries to you,
bringers of joy
and laughter,
rather having met you
than not at all.
I may be small,
but my heart is big.

You swig of the wine.
Supply is there,
taken in care.

Drowned in Me

Of course, I shall begin
with a hello.
How to begin a conversation,
it is the easiest way.
Not by harp or cello
but by word and thought.
Prayerfully I recall you,
your life, and what you do.
Changing beginnings
each and every morning,
each and every time you are
nervous.
Each and every moment,
capturing your elegance,

bringing to light your height,
heady   heights   of
wholesomeness.
Holy, my light in this dim
world,
fighting for each word.
Absurd to think of you used,
abused by sight and standards.
Mangled   and   mindfully
framed.
Maimed by a rush of torrents.
Rains that are so cold
they calm me in the summer.
But winter holds its tongue.
Monetary   uses   subsidiary,
superseded.
They can give,
but it's not this exchange I
live for.
Carrying with you my load.
What note does that?
A note from lover to lover.
My doctor's note,
stating my health and my case.
Free now to begin
with life and your whims.
Carry   me   just   as   you
carried him,
my Christ, my all.
fell but got back up.

Escaping the Draught

There you are.
I see a slight puzzlement.
Your face looks as if
it has been hurt before.
Chance takes itself away.
Storing up dreams
cast aside of the shore,
moments where bleak seems
real.
But you are sealed
by the Holy Spirit,
always in sight of you in him.
My innermost parts are
waiting
for the call to be silent.
Environmental words to
choose from.
Songs we sing are the ones we
show,
shown by its own beating
heart.
Warring nations came aside
as I find the solution.
Hide, my friend.
I will make you a good friend.
Tenderly she waits,
accustomed to advances.

You are the jewel in her crown.
Understand me
as I make my advances,
producing the one
whom I want to dance with.

Felt (Version 1)

My heartfelt cities bring me
to the edge.
The tears are held in a pot
for me
until the release of memories.
The sights empower me to run.
Come home, my friend in my
heart.
This heart is for you to see
no divide; but a friendship
is key.
My felt emotion gone for now.
Somehow I rest in you.
Resting like a chick kept
warm.
Swarming with compliments,
a lot to handle but handled
well.
Coming up trumps is the way
to be.
Come to me, my Son.
I guess you are sent to work,

not as a mechanic, but as a humanitarian,
blessed people with you in the midst.
Kissed tenderly by the ones,
the ones in the midst.
Mysteries told and explained.
For me, you are my water, my life.
And I ought to say about you,
through the threshold,
barriers now gone cold,
safe to pass over.

Fertile

This land of ours,
ploughed and taken up,
sipping the moisture,
a cut above the rest,
calmly sits in pits.
waiting for its taste.
This gate of mine
you come to explore.
My land I find
such a sweet allure.
Before you talk,
before your mind
made up on key,

courtesy I kindly make.
Your colours are still
but fill my head.
Taking that pill
made my head spin.
Calm exterior
facing this world.
This place I see,
is it really for us?
Waiting for the call
to say it is fine.
Masterful memories,
sir, oh so kind.

Fly Me, Try Me

Fly away from troubles at bay.
Kindly consider my ways.
As you praise with hope
in your eyes, I see
the way forward for you and me.
Trees made with ease
to free us from this concrete maze.
Amassed wealth and in good health,
courteously, I say thanks.
All my escapes,

all my days you see,

watching wherever I go.

Certain, in case you didn't know,

knowing how to live

a life of joy and well-being.

The winds are singing your name.

Framed as a masterpiece,

my picture is the same.

Call across, and I shall see

your heart which grows within me.

Averted disgrace from the habit,

it's a new chance,

and I want to have it.

So try me and know me,

here for your love.

The doves are cooing.

Who will be next?

Hope something special

and not in a mess.

Guess that we don't know.

Slowly pacing and reading

about the choices we have.

Are you feeling?

Keep me in mind in your day.

I shall find you.

I love it when you pray

and say those words,

loving daily my case for you.

Deep inside, your love is true.

Food for Thought
(Version 1)

Young, tender heart, one I cannot miss,

you fill my cup and put food in my dish.

For wisdom and knowledge we patiently fish.

Keeping in your heart my taste, my relish.

Speak to me, Father.

Be with me, Lord.

I want to hold you.

Let's see this through.

Feeling my soul, I long for your touch.

I praise your Spirit.

Your words and love mean so much.

Skies above our nation,

led by your hand

in the right direction.
You have a master plan.

Fortune (Version 1)

A noble quest, the crusade, my venture.

Travelling and seeking my mission; to take

the pilgrimage is my searching path.

Deeds alone made a bold escape.

Circumstance and God's will, divine providence my destiny.

My destination brings me here.

Is a marriage in the cards?

Prosperity, productivity, profitability—

you are out in front for gain and success.

Meshes into a strange place,

where we separate but are not separated.

My Sovereign Lord, my King, protector,

magnificent in all your colour.

Exceptionally bright and full of light,

causing spectacular proof of identity.

France (Version 1)

Beloved,

your beauteous, bountiful, blessed purpose arrests my heart.

I start to seduce my splendorous, staggering, shiny stirring.

In me, I see an unerring, timeless, towering, stately home,

Caused in me my abducted, abiding, abandoned place.

When I sing, I bring the joy of life together, elatedly pleasant.

Searching to find a solution to the problem mentioned,

examine yourself, and believe you are worth the call.

Church lurches forward. My star search comes to an end.

As I lift this gift of life called my wife, a fish wife,

holding the rifle, I sense that strain is rife among many.

My fetching, eye-catching verse is real.

Outstretched arms are the outcome of a rule of thumb.

Numb in a sense but drumming on the outside.

Sliding towards the ride of a lifetime,

the resulting urge confers a sequel with a payoff.

Friend in Me

You fill me to the top.

If there is mess, you are the mop.

Sit up, and take heed, my friend.

It's all for you.

Brushing and blowing aside, my enemies trampled underfoot.

We are the lions and lambs.

Come close, and we understand.

Away to those clams and lands.

Of course, we shall support you.

Here in heaven, it is what we do.

Soothing your soul,

your amassed doubts gone in a flicker.

Now that you are well,

I have decided to continue with your choices.

Many hearts, many voices

voicing our mastery and opinion.

Sent on a search for peace in this land.

Sandy beaches robbed.

This land of plenty is getting used.

File a suit to the healthy

that shall make the midday news,

choosing our very own agenda.

Roots running deep,

but never too deep to reach us.

In the pains and struggles,

you find there is none left to battle.

Settled and rested in my nested place,

nesting myself here,

where the voice and hello are sincere.

Grateful

For you are the cause
worth trying for,
worthy of applause,
the curtain call.
Show me the door.
In I walk.
Treasuring your treasure
before and after
the tears, the joy,
the laughter, the boy.
Who is calling you?
Who feeds and nurtures you?
It is I,
my handsome believer,
warrior of peace,
a love-giver.
A round of applause
for my Saviour.
Savouring this moment
of togetherness,
blessed meals
sealed in the Spirit
untainted,
undiminished,
unable to kill.
No hurt caused,

but many applaud.
A reason for
no reason but an excuse,
obtuse and bemused.
Come to me.
I want to use you
in a mighty way.

Help

Our help is at home,
where time is a healer.
Tease out of me
and my sealed lips
the truth, my truth,
a mix of lies and tales,
relentlessly wanting more,
as I saw to my discredit.
Mention the truth of me,
and I run and hide.
Because in my disguise,
I feel free
but bare and open.
Vulnerability and fear
rock me sometimes.
Where there is sight
but others who are blind,
carefully walk

when they should run,
running ahead of the
competition.
It's the way things are
coursing through my veins.
Blood is a life-giver,
but sometimes I shiver,
quivering like a feather
in the wind.
Close by is my friend,
who ends the fantasy
to good effect.

Hold on Tight

Furthermore, to your question
of life in deleted detention,
mention my habitat of hope
and joy.
Of course, I am here
and always will be
because I, your Father and
friend,
will keep you from all terror.
By day and by night, I am the
protector,
protection for the light
and an enemy of the darkness.
Forced into labour,

the tides are spinning and
turning.
Cause for hope
I share with you, my love.
Hold on tight to the covenants,
the ones I make with my
children.
Stating your very case,
I see your colours,
like a peacock in full vigour.
My years and your tears.
I give your heart a rest.
Caught me in full dress,
but undressed are your wants.
But dressed beautifully are
my dreams.
With you I wish to share,
needing your stance to stand.
Keep me searching for level
ground.
The sound of a thousand larks
playing a thousand harps
on two thousand legs—
minus a few lost in the rain.
Again, I tend to their needs.
Crumbling walls
measured.

Holding Me Together

Cement the binding force
strong as rain.
Divorced being forced
into the cupboard,
cornered and ill.
We go in your will,
setting the goals of life.
Not moving posts
but keeping a close look.
Demands are hard for
marriage.
Settled now.
No carrying carriages.
My wantings and needings,
breeding and feeding.
Children a blessing,
but only with feeling.
This bonding talk,
walking the walk of saints.
Battle won, and we don't wait
for blessings to come.
Take what is given you
with a thankful heart,
not separated but at peace.
My tender son,
why don't you weep?

How I Dine

First, let me tell you
I committed a crime.
Totally wasted
and washed out on wine,
coming to you
sorrowful.
May I borrow another yesterday?

Rude and limited,
Mindly decisions halted,
did rather than didn't.
To the past
I dedicated my mistakes,
dedicating a new era
to my lover,
where undercover,
she works on me.

Free from sin and drink,
my success is clear.

On the brink of discovery,
on the brink of greatness,
on the brink of happiness.

Close to my father,
and close to you.

I Am Your Vessel (Version 1)

Fill me with your water.
Come to me with your hope
for every son and daughter.
Tug my heart with your rope
and rescue me.

Pour, pour, pour me out.
No mounting pressure shall
rise.
Pour, pour, pour me out.
Oh, to see you in my eyes.

Lord, you are my keeper,
my ever hope in trouble.
Lord, you are my healer.
Keep me in your trusted
bubble.

Pour, pour, pour me out.
No mounting pressure shall
rise.
Pour, pour, pour me out.
Oh, to see you in my eyes.

Pour, pour, pour me out.

No mounting pressure shall
rise.

Pour, pour, pour me out.

Oh, to see you in my eyes.

I Gave You Life (Version 1)

Property and quality
distinguish growth.

The life I gave you is reproduced
in your environment.

Your mental state is like
metal,

unable to shift or break.

Put on your brakes for rest
and settle.

Born, I had to warn you of
certain scorn

as you were torn from society
and friendship.

I am always here to lend an ear.

Severe situations but total
reconciliation.

Bearing fruit, I cradle you
with my pillow.

Soft and lovely is your
embrace.

In me, you have yielded a crop of plenty.

I blossom in keeping to your plan

for my life you have me by the hand.

Your land is in your heart,

and no one can remove it from you.

I Receive of You
(Version 1)

Calling you mine is a lovely way to see

your efforts bursting beyond sea waves.

Courteously, you left with no damage.

My search for you is now complete.

Sensing you now, my job has come.

My job for you to reason and begin,

to stare humanity in the face

and say, 'I love my God, and he loves me.'

Nothing they do can part us.

I am in you, with you, and part of you.

Nothing high or low, to or fro, nor distance nor pace nor face.

I place you in high regard.

I know it's hard to be you,

and it's a shame to see you reduced.

It's hard when I search for you.

You kindly whisper in my ear,

'I am always there, and I care.

You can speak to me and share with the brothers in your care.

I lift you up, so rejoice in me.

And cling to my promises.

I want your attention.'

I saw You

Beyond the river that will rise,

burst its bank, and called me over,

sensing a Christlike urgency,

I delved and dug into the muddy waters.

A tree of a ripe old age,

sharing its taste and faithful free.

You saw me lay down, and weeping you said,

'I am here for you; don't be misled

Your head is clear, and your space is near,

close to a quenchable thirsty water.

Clear to the onlookers

shook by the gallant waves.'

Hazy, lazy days found out in his waiting,

penetrating as oil waiting for his words.

Seeking my toll to warm the cold air.

I am there and always will be.

I saw you gaze at me through a clear glass,

the filling and chilling taste

enough to cause a stir,

stirring inside my massive late lunch.

Crusty, crunchy leaves left torn and bare.

Life had gone from its crustation.

Sensational reports distorting the truth.

'Where are you when I ask?

And there I see you, bright as the stars,

stars in distance to see

your pining eyes. Are they for me?'

Lay Me Down

This hollow life of hollow floors

turns my answers into wantings.

Of course, it is my turn

to take the weight and its flaws.

Coming to you, I trust you are well.

Turn mourning into dancing.

Still looking for the one,

the one your heart sings for,

the one you secretly long for.

Cast out the worries

and declare your life a success.

Monumental I find your cause,

a case to replace my heavy thoughts

caught in a drift,

where my answers live.

Life is for your living.

Oh, what a wonderful gift.
Case made in the jury and
court.
Time is beginning,
sorted into order,
where there are no visible
borders.
This is the case I make,
searching for my Father's
sake.
Create a vision of hope.
Walking that mountain,
what a dangerous slope.
Coping with the deep mud.
The swinging wind,
lay me down
and colour me with your
flowers,
understood to be good.
And my service to be
well received
because I believe you love me.
And that's all I need to know.

Leeds station

Meeting the nation
at Leeds Station,
carry my liaison

as I speak with you.

Bigger than many,
this town I see.
Fortune goes with us,
going back to
our mother place,
touching base.

Ornate in standing,
understanding the race,
the race for my place
on this train.
My pain has gone.
Waiting for us
in our midst,
he came to give
and give direction
to a place from
Leeds train station.

Mind over Matter

It is all in the mind,
clattering and shouting.
It is me; I am here,
steering the ship.
Along with my wind,

I carry the vessel
on the way to victory.

The war was on.
Guns were poised for eruption.
But ours were left at home.
The enemy ship,
that ship of destruction,
was swallowed up whole.
The ocean smashed it
and tore out its power.

We went home
to safety and peace.
Along came my friend,
who love will never cease.
This vessel of hope and joy
caused my inward soul to cry,
crying in love's beauty,
this home we call ours.
Surrender to the cause;
your services are needed.
I shall take you there
without a fuss.
Injustice needs change,
and hope needs a page
for memories.

Mine Is Yours (Version 1)

The course of this journey felt
encased in a special, pure
felt.
It's because of you I sing,
making everything in good
supply.
Sunset to sunrise, I see the
skies.
They laugh when they see me,
majestic in their ways.
Come to me; I shall show you
all the awesome promises.
I keep for you for your growth.
Enough to bring me tears of
the years
spent   nurturing   you,
blessing you.
Your fortification enough to
mention.
My   prayers   and   cares   to
keep you,
to keep you young and brave.
My boldness I share with you,
encased in a little shiny gift.
The box you see opened,
my son, I opened for you.
You receive wisdom.

Father, you are mine, and I am yours.

I pause for a moment, and I think of your smile.

Bless you, my son, my love.

My Course (Version 1)

My course you do directs me to hope.

Home to my keeping, no weeping.

Wept for the girl showed you care.

May I offer you some good advice?

I feel you are a little paranoid.

Come to me, and hear my voice.

The comings and goings are directed,

connected to the cause of no divorce.

Seeing you happy and smiling keeps me awake.

I think of you.

I dream of your confidence in me.

You show it sometimes.

But, of course, doubts arise.

Seeing proof, we see your need.

But for you, it is easy to believe.

And that's what I want and need.

So breathe this air I give you.

Believe you are loved and can also

breathe with me as I lay to rest.

Not ever second best I feel you.

You treat me as I should be treated.

With love and respect, you scored.

My Father | (Version 1)

My Son, do not depart from me.

I have much to say

and so little time to do so.

Being with you and watching you

bring me years of tears.

You cry, but you don't know how.

You see, but you don't perceive.

You talk, but it's not complete.

You think occasionally, and that is fine.

Bring yourself some respect and love.

The corner you turned was for me.

You come to me not knowing what to do.

I feel for you and your struggles.

I feel for you and your pain.

Your emotions not felt.

And your prosperity is good for me.

From me I see your smile.

The mile you have walked is hard,

and the love you seek is somewhere.

But here it is perfect.

Searching for that breath of air,

someone to rock your world,

be sensible, and pick wisely.

You have the knowledge now

to make a lasting change.

Keep turning the page, and you will find

the one your heart desires.

My Guarded Heart

I see you over there

with golden locks.

A strong will prepared.

Stare at me; I want to see

the realms you find me in.

Purposefully floating on promises,

the ones you impart to me, to us.

Freeing the kind souls

who fell along the way,

tortured and tormented.

We have our day

when we pray to reach.

The outward-seeking face

looks straight in me.

There are no fears.

When we render here,

somewhat dismayed and out of place,

beware my God is there,

certainly taking the force

and ramming it in the bin,

where sin is gone.

Giving in to my tasks

that run wide,

to catch them, I know

my guarded heart
has to grow.

My Little Prayer

Seeing you in your poverty,
you became poor for us,
so we can become rich
in your glory.
With the glory
assigned to you,
holding you in my arms,
I feel a certain charm.
Disarming you was simple;
it is your wish.
Fishing around for truth,
for a suitable home
which I found in you.
Rains that fall
are no problem for you,
sent to release us,
to give us a future
of hope and a nurturing
Spirit.
Keep me living in you.
I will remain in you
if you remain in me.
Touching base,

I sense a positive change
where age doesn't matter
and wealth has no place
amongst us.
Tussling for it
is a waste of time
as I shall show you.

My Plans Are for Your Good (Version 1)

Timothy, let me know how
you feel.
Let me know what you do.
Feel my loving nature
surround you.
Of course, I want the best
for you,
and I give you understanding.
My friend and neighbour
flies,
flies like a spinning top at
full height.
Your stature keeps me
inside you.
I wonder about you to benefit
your mind.
The loving-kindness I need
you to know,

courses you take throughout your days,

that nights are OK for you.

You have grown strong and straight—

right up until the final call—

making a difference wherever you go.

I go out and shout your name.

I go in and call you in.

I create your very soul renewed daily.

You are calm now; I reach for you.

sometimes I know, bring and sow

countless days in your wonder.

I care for you, my beautiful wonderboy.

My Prayer (Version 1)

I taught you to see and believe.

In you, my answers are lived.

Forgive and forget; let out your net.

Blessings galore to be in your arms.

Teach me to have and to hold.

My plantations are now in your grasp.

You grasp what others struggle to.

My house has many rooms.

I shall prepare a place for you.

To have and to hold you

in my arms; I rescue you from it all.

I call, and if anyone answers,

I will welcome them into my abode.

The water is sweet to taste,

And nothing is made in haste.

No ruin shall befall you,

none of the powers of darkness.

I have named you; you are mine,

and I find in you peace and tranquillity.

I have measured you, and you are whole.

No bitter bruises; your fruits are tasty.

Praise on your lips I feel from you.

Your calm exteriors multiply your favour.

Think of me as your neighbour,

your loving Saviour.

My Trying to Please
(Version 1)

The course we ran and walked.

Pain is gone now, as you can see.

I clearly let you know your role,

where clarity suddenly unfolds the truth.

Merciful, you are my dear Lord.

Searching for something close,

a dose of reality, sensing my purpose.

Nervous not to see you, but to wait

for you, I take down strongholds.

For you, I bring down powerful enemies.

For you, I keep in your heart of hearts.

In my mind, I realize for sure

you are wanted, made, and kept pure.

Feeling your heart makes me happy.

Being with you on your journey,

deservedly so, is my one I bring

to keep you safe, kept in me.

My Spirit enfolds you to see

all the things you want to be.

And, of course, things aren't always right.

But now you are calm and safe.

Safe in her arms and mine

because love is sweet,

fit for my soul,

my Comforter, my joy.

My Wealth I Bless
upon You (Version 1)

I teach you my customs.

You do transpire,

short of strength but high in me.

Fortunately, I bless myself,

as do the rest of us.

In good health you sing to me

as my fortune runs its course.

For you, my love will always remain.

Trains come and go,

stop and start.

My love is always at the station,

waiting for you to take a step of faith.

Board the plane; the pain is all gone.

Begin to know I am for you.

I sweep, I clean, I try.

For my love is always in good supply.

Translate for me your words.

Your language I wish to learn.

this burning love never goes out.

It's that warmth I need from you.

Taste me, and see I am sweet.

My levels never drop or decrease

because you sing, and it's all for me.

Treat her well, and you shall see

a bride encompassing understanding.

The dream may be cheap, but I keep you

safe in all sincerity.

Bless you.

On the Train

Oh, the journey.

One doth complain.

Burly men

onwards to my place

of comfort, of choice.

Oh, train, hear my voice.

Make some noise

as my opinions do count.

Surmountable pressures

gestured forward

towards your opinion.

My opinion stays put

as the engine drags,

shoves, and pulls.

Unmistakable by nature,

is it natural

to want to sit silent?

Silence is smothered,

covered in glitter

as my Father is.

His voice I know well.

Come to me, my Father,

and deliver me.

The journey, my destination,

I feel frustration

that you won't feel

or know.

Partake of Matter

Subject matter
hard to define.
Scatter your words.
They are good
seeds grown.
Of grace you are known.
Throne of the righteous,
home for might.
Sightly gaze,
a kindly phrase,
praising together for
our Lord and Father.
Rather, his words
than the company of other
replacing   thoughts   with
words.
I see your point and sense
the fence has come down,
blown in the wind.
Certainly we chase
our friends, not defaced
or erased or complacent.
Placing your adjacent corners
through the reaches of the
earth.
Deservedly so.

No worries of tomorrow.
The bringer of days is here.
With you I sense a purpose.
Don't be nervous.
The money is surplus.

Playfully I Rise

Rising without intent,
every corner and shade,
I shall reveal its weight.
Encountering   your
counterparts,
slay the dragon,
and there are a few.
Where we shall begin
and give it its due?
Your words are strong.
You belong with us.
Careful as you go.
Be giving without fuss.
Trust in me, the Lord,
and you shall blossom
into the most beautiful dance
I have ever seen.
Believe me when I say
your days are numbered.
Come here and pray

for love, for hope, for joy.
Boys need a father,
and I am choosing you.
Carefully consider
your future queen and King.
Sing to me,
and you do sing beautifully.
Study and listen.
It's going so well.
Flying high above the stars
in ways you excel.
Water my goats.
Feed my sheep.

Clean me, and keep me clean.
I shall ponder your Word.
Your ways are far above mine,
but humble enough to share
kindly your communion
with me.
Thanks, and many thank
yous.
I searched, wondered, and
pondered,
and there you are,
right here in and with me.
We shall go far enough
to live together.
Life and all its gifts
surrender me to the cause.

I shall keep you happy.
Search me and find your
home.
Kissing my feet and deserving
of love,
cause for concern gone.
This is home
and where you belong.

Refugee (Version 1)

I was lurching and
self-searching,
researching my strip searcher,
nurturing my sister.

Come over, my chum, but
don't lay the crumbs.
Living glum inside a slum,
the tables turn.

Found my mound; the sound
is gowned.
Astounded by your wounded,
earthbound rocket
pocketing the tip box
contents,
of the key to his lover's box.

Pick up the pieces, and make
a timepiece.

Release my lease from greasy fingers.
Your hairpiece caught a press release.

Furthermore, I came to bear your chore
for the smut-shaking closed door.
First floor's downpour the sense of my décor.

Scattered

Does it really matter
that we pause and think?
That sinking feeling,
feeling on the brink.
Where lovers meet,
freedom awakens my soul.
Knowledge brought forward.
No awkward silences banned.
Banishes the tarnishing sounds.
Breaking point.
We have come so far.
No cause lost
in my Abba's eyes,
causing us to think.
<u>S</u>ink comfortably

into your own chair.
Where has chaos gone?
Lost in the wind.
My appointment nearing,
cheering and no jeering.
Capable of much,
such as the grass is green.
It grows, and it knows it's time.
Job done and on the move.
Grooves crafted from his mood.
He twinkles and sparkles.
The larks sing an inclining feeling
of the just that are likened
to my darling thrush,
rising and diving
because they love to sing.
Bring me praise.
I shall enter and serve
my dessert for you.
It shall be sweet,
and we will greet each other.
Love doesn't die,
and that is why
I eat humble pie.

Scented Flower

Calling on you,
you are my Master.
Sent in a rush,
plaster my cracks
to hide the failings
of hideous proportions.

Mention me while you're
here,
calming your new year,
fearing nothing but loss.
You are here now,
and you are the boss.
<u>Stirring</u> and changing,
not middle-ageing.
Instead, you'll find me
praising,
praying in person.
Lying on the soft green grass
of another country.
How sweet to wake
with the sun on your face.
Carefully awake to find
all is OK.
Running away was my way
of gaining control.
Sauntered and wandered,

you never fell.
And you never will.
Still the waters.
You shall find questions
in your mind and answered.
Stay calm and clear.
It's a race worth winning.
Be of good cheer; I am here.

Secreto

I secretly want you,
your style and point of view.
Cascading and rearranging.
A straightforward question?
Give me some time
to think it over.
You are sweet and pretty,
but it doesn't last—
in my sight anyway.
Throw caution to the wind,
the bending and blowing
wind.
Secretly I want you,
but I am scared.
Let it not happen again
to me, to us.
I am fortunate to be here

and sincerely blessed
with hope in my chest.
Guarded to take what's
thrown.
My own secrets.
I no longer choose to share.
Buried in my emotional mess,
guess what it is?

Amazed at the sound
of your voice; you share
where you plot our steps.
You take us with you.
You take us there.
Staring into the distance,
and it is all yours
to play with.

Send Us

Bend us and nurture us.
We believe in you,
and you we shall trust.
Cautionary departures
guided to the One
who made the heavens.
Our dreams, our lives, our
breaths.
His vigour and power are
eternal.
Nocturnal choirs sound
asleep.
Deep is the ocean.
Carry me still.
Secrecy and delicacy used.
Brethren accused of wrongs;
taken lightly our serious
case.

Stable Diet

You are my diet, Father.
You are my daily portion.
I come to you,
not just in need, but in want.
I see what you do
and what you create.
My Father, I want you,
to see you,
to touch you
in a perfect love
only you can give.
Simmering ideas of hope,
choosing to be
my meal.
Taking me on an exciting way.
Feeding on you, I pray
for me to feel.

<u>Carry me forth.</u>
<u>Reinvent the wheel.</u>
Share with me the meal
of remembrance,
of taste,
of sweet nourishment
further to my health,
my wealth of knowledge,
my richness in character.
You build my future
and my present.
My past, we think of
all the love and the drama.
Good times.

Stay

Caught in a dazy gaze.
The neighbours are plotting,
for sure.
Protests a little leg shown.
They went for the old ways.
But now, it has all gone,
the shining from my eyes.
A surprising thought occurs
to a passing gentleman:
Where has dignity gone?

Where is kindness?
Where are our homes?

Smashed to smithereens
by our adversary.
It won't last.

As a man of will,
searching for answers
to questions no one asked,
I speak to you on a level
where a treble measure
found beneath my feet
cure the lame
and made the weak strong.
This gentleman,
tired and weary,
has discovered hope,
a lasting hope,
gripping onto every morsel,
making it his own.
Embedded in his heart
a throne of joy.
'Victory,' I say
to the boy who says it all.

Take Me Home (Version 1)

The basement I found myself in,

a place of self-assessment.

I replaced my mind inside

previously interlaced problematics,

encased within my own face.

To be traced, I placed race

where aerospace came to my rescue.

Your grace helped to keep me young.

Birthplace humble but still a showplace.

No disgrace in living by suitcase,

although you needed not.

Heart protected in chrome.

Shalom and peace the antidote.

Honeycomb for food-vacated moon.

My syndrome staying home.

I rid myself of leaving and grieving.

Believing and perceiving

the thieves are tied up.

Conceiving the weaving of the muck.

There are no overachievers,

and an underachiever breaks through.

Take Notice

Brothers and sisters in the faith

caught me a place to rest.

I searched and probed for something,

fishing for answers

in a callous way for me.

Justified alongside my day,

where happy meadows play.

The wind that day was fresh.

Food was too good to turn down.

And there you are.

Your folk should be respectful.

I wonder if they are.

You have come far,

but somehow, they do not notice.

Your elegance, your poise.

Why so strange?

I was with you for years,

taking the blows,

being measured up,

doubting and debating.

You could have cut me,

but the serrated edge turned,

turned on its user.

No pain caused; no bruise formed.

No deformity, only scars.

You were a part of my journey.

Come and be careful.

Don't just stare

or look right through me.

I am here in person,

just as you are.

So begin a change

in their hearts, and show my state.

My age and merits want to be shown.

Maturity and humility accepting

apologies if they are formed even in the mind.

Tenderly You Turn Me (Version 1)

You turn me around for the one.

I come to see you even when you do wrong.

You see me, and I think of you.

The courts are waiting to have you.

We see always the delight you bring.

Feeling my certainly dense feeling,

dense in a work likened to strength.

Your weekends are empty,

waiting to be filled with joy.

Certainly takes me away

from the pain of the land.

Inhabitants from afar come to me,

waiting to have what you have.

They struggle and strive

to live a life pleasing to me.

But for us, it is easy—

no pressure, no pain, no ache.

I sense your fears through the years

of emotional torment and vulnerability.

Go into the country,

where I sense your curiosity.

Mention me when you are there,

and I shall bless you abundantly.

Not always in words do I thank you.

The Course I Take

(Version 1)

My miniature being comes close to glory.

But come to me, and I will tell you a story.

Caught in my very reasonable state,

my very stature comes at a greater price.

My Saviour, my home, my peace.

Thank you, Lord, for your giving nature.

It's me I see when I look at you.

So come to me, and I shall give you rest.

Never second best, but my cloak hides me,

hides my confidence and my very being.

The cloak gives a false sense of attention.

Too many times it's so hard to mention.

The Course

Finding in your room,

like a tomb full of collections,

but they will not come with you.

As you reveal to this passing illusion

that what you need is bought

ought to be free of stuff.

It is not your identity.

Friends speak not of wealth.

You are a rich man, indeed,

when you have your health.

Elatedly rich with vigour

and deemed fit to be a giver.

I quiver as you say to me,

'I want you.'
Not to be seasonally present
means no end to me.
As I flutter around
purposefully,
bright in the knowledge,
as I stir my porridge,
knowledge I have gained
to obtain the truth,
hidden secrets come out in
the open.
A notion to count surmounting
cost.
You paid the cost for me
as I watch you intimately.
Purposely, in an instant,
working on my mind
entwined with hope,
muscling hard as you work.
It is all for our benefit
to be gifted
with a soft, calm, watery
voice.
Your choice and your voice
to show
my knighted and wanting
hope.

The New Way

Finally I can say
all I want to say.
Bring me venture
an education,
experience,
adventure.

Finally I can be
all I want to be.
Steady and strong,
began talking,
walking,
head up high.

Finally I can breathe.
Easy does it/
Exhale,
inhale,
direction.

Finally I win
as I took part,
survived,
cried my tears.
Years of struggle,
and now I am free.

Think of You (Version 1)

Conceive, ideate, concoct,
hatch, fashion, fabricate.
Forming the ideals of my life
here on this planet.

That sinking feeling where
all thoughts are clinking.
The home I carefully tidy.
My comb brushes through all
tangles and twinings.
Syndromes are created through
home dwellings.

But you are the reliable one,
chewing through the meat,
releasing the fat.
Swallowing whole, you grew
to receive.
Spewing the impurities like
I knew you would.
Truly, you are the one whose
views are my safety.

Wondering words are shaped
into form.
A configuration, construct,
skeleton, frame.
an acclaimed piece of mastery
in sync.

With the mystery of change
and inner thought,
inside me I feel at peace.

What a sight

Politely I begin
with the staring caught
under the chin.
Laughing and smiling,
grinning with delight.
Courts answer your plea
to be free from harm.
And it is true what I am told,
that you are honest and bold,
relinquished of control,
living your life,
not out of age.
old enough to know
to be careful of whom
you show your heart to.
You amuse me with your wit.
Does anyone else get it?
Promises you rarely make.
And try to make no mistake,
carefully as you go
into this world made with
love.

Forms the shapes
of every dove there is.
Pleases me to see
shifting away from hurt.
You deserve the best.
You deserve me
honestly never to deprive you
of all your seeds sewn
for your benefit.

A Loose Cannon

Load it until it is silly
stuffed, little boy.
The walk is so hilly.
Not your little toy
to play with as you like.
I am a man, so please
understand,
with caring hands I carry out
my plans.
Started something big and
real.
One day I am counted
one of the few.
Does not compute.
The answer to the question
gives me help,
gives me a mention.

Taught to live high and wide.
Your supply is high to the
heavens.
You shall not die but live.
This is my gift to you,
for you.
With limitless help and
understanding,
your well is full.
I will not hide you;
you are my chance to show
all I am
tied in one little bow.
Take and shoot.
We are rooting for you.
Do my bidding, and you
shall be
held in honour and courage,
you see.
Tied and belted up,
safe in this way.

A Mixed Bag

Sometimes when I play,
it can fill my whole day.
There are instruments
and all sorts of fun.

I always come back to
number 1,

my Lord and carer,

teacher and friend.

Sent to solve the problem

of a bend in the law.

More of what I need

rather than what I want.

It's a mixed bag, this life.

Carry me further on.

We won the race.

Now, let's start at a moderate
pace.

I love seeing you smile.

And that look on your face.

You call us to serve.

In us no disgrace.

A sound mind plans and digs

For the right place.

Water released from its captors.

Above the sea

Certain harmonies,

crystallising images,

peaceful balances of life.

Humanity is being tugged
and pulled

in directions I don't want
them to go.

Caramelized in their shelters

they call their homes.

Come to me for you are mine.

I own you, but not disown you.

You are mine, and come
summertime,

I'm treating you to my
sunshine.

Slipping away carefree and
hungry,

you dip in the water.

While floating carefully

but above the water, you sing

gentle harmonies which
bring me joy

to the edge of my seat.

Come with me, and we
shall fly,

eating the food kings eat.

The anointed one comes to my
attention.

Someone here wants to give
you a mention.

Your strength gives me peace
of mind.

All of Me

Shouting above the waves,
I feel you stir.
Birds soar high,
but under the sea, I see
changes that follow
under my feet,
causing me to feel.
Come over.
I want you
to be the steel
which is unbending.
Sending you to my ways.
Caught a glimpse of you.
Staff on holiday pay,
care to be my breeze?
Easy to be counted.
Shirts creased and wet.
Use the machine?
I am no veteran.
Answers are there;
you need to listen.
A big wide world,
hiding only pains me.
As I come down from earth,
The undeserved and
underpaid

raise their glasses.
Honour comes to those who
wait.
Wait for me; I am worth it.
All the miserable lovers
have a place somewhere in
my heart.
I count to ten, and they are
still there.
Hear me as I declare
this man is open and not
broken.

Ambushed

I never knew who you were.
For all I knew, you weren't.
But I see you next to me.
Opened the key to my heart.
The life we share
we have to declare the peace.
Abundantly blessed from
afar.
Here I know you.
Seeing your design,
looking for a way in,
sitting and looking
for the piece I desired.

Searching and finding the one
I can be myself with,
Teething and feeling our way,
we come together.
Two by two,
the covenant we share
answers all my questions.
we need to mention.
Got to pay attention.
Ambushed I was,
but in a good way.
Some say my heyday has left.
But honey, I'm just getting started.

As If by Chance

Changes are good for the summer.
But in the winter, we hold on,
hold on to our memories.
Set me free from the frosty shivers.
Mostly paint, but I ain't a quitter.
Shimmering in the sun,
my holiday was fun.
Call me up for an adventure.

After my new book
and my sentiments are clear,
Sergeant, I am not welcome
as I fear the terrors of the night.
It would be a mistake
to have me lead your operation.
I would outsmart myself
And end up in circles.
Is it OK for me to work that way?
Quitter by night
and stopping by day.
Come to mine, and I'll show you how
the bruises mend.
And your men will say
Thank you, dear sergeant.
We want to go that way.

Be Counted

A wise one, I count you in.
Precious Son. Let's begin.
Ladders, I see them
strutting their stuff,
showing their tough exteriors.
In honesty, I bring to thee
My total and utter reliability.

Count me in.

I am on a mission path.

Gasps of air came with me

just to show my rigid notions.

Pity the person who has a fright.

Not going up there,

Especially by night.

Further still,

send me the bill.

Free ride from new,

now and forever.

Clever little ones

caught up in their guns.

Sons and daughters

Beyond what I see.

Birthday Cheer

Darling, be of good cheer.

Looking for you,

I found you here.

Searching for your tear,

emotion in me gone.

But I know where I am from.

Come over and celebrate.

Another year to commemorate.

Mental state healthy;

you brought me through.

Your youth searched my heart,

coming together.

Oh well, I never.

It's your day.

Hoping I haven't let you down

surrounding you with my all.

I try, but my God is bigger.

Filling your need,

he bled for us.

Central to me you are.

I want to lift you up.

A supper of cake always good.

Understand I am only one man.

Holding my hand, you swoon.

Of course, I can.

By Ear

I can hear you when you bring me

close to the brink I need to see.

Blood pumping through my veins.

Up to my ear, I sense a saint.

Come by here, and lend me one.

Staggered and shattered,

come and bear my son.

He needs the reins to begin his run.

Friendship tells me you are my guy.

I come to thee and sanctify.

When on my shoulders. I cry for your safety.

Maybe, oh maybe, it's raining.

Out there it is cold and dank.

But here with us, you have a home

to roam as you will.

The tone beyond what I could not sense.

On the earth, I repent of my sins.

Believe me when I say,

'You have come a very long way.'

Waves and winds call me home to

my heavenly Father, with his arms wide open.

By the Window

The station pauses for air.
Here again,
I sit in the same old chair.

I get on the train.
Sit close to the window.
Must maintain the sorrow
of inadequacy.
I see her
right in the corner.
The reflection in my window,
searching for her eyes.
She turns and looks.
A lovely surprise.
I see your sky
As I lie down on my nice bed,
disguising my pain
and the pain in my head.
Keeping it all together,
I replace the suffering
with muffled muffling,
shuffled shuffling.
No cause for alarm.

Call Me, I Am Here

To hear your voice,
I have no choice but to listen.
I have a choice
to tending my ear towards your call.
There is love in you still,

although you feel nothing
at all.
You make for me my meal.
I readily cherish a well-
cooked one.
Becomes part of me
to nurture and for gain.
Your Spirit in me
surfing my hidden depths.
Emotion causing the ocean
to spit and well up inside.
Undercurrents supply our
force.
Don't be dragged under.
Or plunder my treasure!
For some around me
care not for me at all.
Wonderful to have a waterfall.
Tall wonders shorten me
as the burden is lifted.

and recue the day?
But at night, it is hard to see.
So much loss.
But in the day, there is life
and light.
Sometime in between
there is a gasp
coming right from the sea.
Seems bottomless and vast.
It's only straight down.
No need to ask direction.
It is right there.
No need to look
for signs and trodden paths.
No urgency but to be carried
along.
This nearly invisible force
caused me to add to my ways.
No more tripping pavements
or end of days.

Calm in the Ocean

Certain motions on this trepid
journey
brought to pass my lost
memory.
If I were to lose my way,
would my ship come

Calm

When all is silent,
choirs call and vibrate.
Vibrant shows alleviate the
loneliness.
But only for a while.
Silence is golden when risen.

Blemished are the prison walls.
The halls soundless
Until lunch comes.
Boundless boundaries
kept and hidden
inside the mental division.
Forcibly noticed amongst staff.
Keeping order,
escaping the border,
found by lawgivers.
Serve your time and learn
is the wisest way to go.
Addiction born out of loss,
tossing away control,
morals loose.
They seem free to abuse.
The noose doesn't fit.

Cast No Shadow

I caught a glimpse in the mirror.
Sought answers for my tears.
Nearing the end of my dinner,
my fears forced out by my Lord.
Surfacing towards the dusty shores,
shadows facing me.
I cast none.
I'm on my own.
The battle is won
By my varied tonal implements.
Seafarers' coincidence.
As I rush to the finish,
diminished but nearly home,
I let down my guard.
The pounding I took
was of significance in my life.
Journeys misspelt.
Names cracked by taste.
Another win for us.
Facing the face of our winner,
Lord Jesus Christ,
we see no better hero.

Caught by the Catcher

Fishing for your lunch,
a bunch of hardy workers
gather on the pier,
start to mention
that way of life.
I cut the line
to start again.

Good thing I brought
my fisherman's friend.
The rigs I barely know.
Hands are tied.
I stopped going,
but I shall return again
withfreshlymadestrengthand
patience to listen.
Those tips I am given,
put them into practice.
I know my lines.
I have written them many
times.
Stretched and taut,
I feel a catch.
Then I realized
fish should either be in the
sea or on your plate.

Change

There is something inside me
that wants to be free.
But I know that to describe me,
you need to be by the sea.
Courteously you call twice.
Found in your garden,
a riotous voice shouts, 'Hey!'

Before I knew what happened,
they were off and away.
Caught in the draft,
drivers blocked my path.
Change wants to happen.
It will come in half,
half an hour, half an ounce.
Try me at times,
counting the steps,
steps up to higher ground.
Change puts me in a daze
when all I want to do
is refrain.
Caught in the rain,
seems like the start all over
again.

Come Over

The wishy-washy flavours of
yesterday
made me think and learn
and play.
Come over to my land I call
home,
where comfort is real and
normal.
Cast aside your nets and bows.

The food you need is wildly grown.

In a zone of head-made plans,

the music you are looking for

was brought hand in hand.

Touching the floor is such a drag

when you are tall.

Come to mine,

where football is fun and free.

No injury here, and there is fair play.

Goals and saves not of this world.

There are gasps of victory and honour.

This game of yours,

oh, what a wonder.

Left me to ponder love and rules,

certain to find your best jewels.

Wisdom we need and feel.

Jointly taken out for a good meal.

Courtesy of My Wife

We came together

pitied and somewhat shy.

Battles we were in

took us on a certain ride.

Cannot believe my eyes.

Wise and fair,

came in to my sight.

'I want to see your light.

Damsel to have and to hold,

courtesy of your match.'

Made a good one here.

Both a good catch.

Furthermore, I rest my case.

My dear children,

don't go in haste.

Let us talk a little,

erase sadness from your mind.

It's all good now.

So I leave you my peace.

Fairly and calmly together,

never leave me.

We care for you both

of the cloth.

Certain to make host.

Delighted guests,

you see them both.

Dry

Call me if I can't see
the trouble surrounding me.
Fortified castles break loose.
We are moving again.
But I won't tell you where
until the day is dying.
I will walk you there,
bearing up under the strain.
Come to me; I need to remain.
Certain tasks need to be
by sight and by ear.
Search me for I am hope.
Find me for I am your eyes.
Surprising when I come to think
about your growth,
linking love with life.
You come to me; no need to think twice.
Kites fly me to the moon
when love is in bloom.
Far cry from when I was pushed,
ushered home.
I found my pulse.

Emergence

Surge emerged on top.
I was underneath and lost the plot,
not to be an announced pleasure.
Measureless the bounty of love.
Striving, straining
to be what she needs.
Paving a way.
Kindly liked to tease.
Wanting all day to caress her.
I emerged wilfully faint
as the law was just
when it said you can't.
Her stance a shaking beauty,
elegant and sultry.
No need for money.
We come to you
taunted and bare.
Hounded for hours,
I was there with you.
Come with me, and I shall show you
timeless, classical moments of bliss.
Will I ever find from this

ways to kiss in this extreme?

Counsel you to your full potential?

Maid of honour?

Yes, I have to mention

your colour, warm and bright.

I see in you

such a culinary delight.

Fellows of the Wind

I sometimes hear you howling.

But rarely I hear you singing.

We used to play.

It was so much fun.

What happened to my friend

when you revealed who you are?

Hearing your call,

like sweet lips forming words,

in my ear I found you

sometimes dry or wet.

Carrying me is a safe bet.

Blow me over as you show

power in your smile.

Growing in stature and confidence,

please let us make amends.

Where you reign in sight

of a world striving to do right.

We need to trust in you

And not by works.

Your power, my guardian,

will solve our problems.

Sob for the world.

Filtered

Water catches our imaginations.

What is it?

Why is it so important?

It brings us spiritual cleansing.

Furthermore, there is no end.

Its horizon changes constantly.

Not to mention its functionality.

Tears worn on the sleeve,

salty, salty tears.

Meant to cleanse years of hurts,

filtering my sadness into life.

Come to me, my love,

and I will never think twice.

The stove is nice and warm.

Baking your specialty,

hidden until the eyes see

a wonderful surprise to be,

nurtured and faithfully made.

Murmured and constant in its ways.

Hazy days left my sugar in the tea.

Couldn't afford the dentistry.

Judgements made and given.

Finding the Way

We look for what is unseen

beneath our very own breaths.

Searching but not aware

of the times we find ourselves in.

Brought to the light barren consequences.

My pot is full, but my purse is empty.

Plentiful of blessings at home.

Roaming, we pretend we are not seen.

But believe me when I say

pure of heart and a life of serenity

get us through when we look to thee.

We find our ways of knowing,

loving the truth, and overflowing in grace.

Parchment sent for the winners' race.

The crown soon to follow.

Purchased by our Lord for us to see

true beauty who loves and lives,

and lives to love our souls.

We are protected wherever we go

and wherever we stay.

Rest is with us, and sense follows close by.

Yearning for an answer and wired to believe.

His whole sense of being

made known, and we are keen to understand

handmade scriptures inspired by our loving Holy Spirit,

taught us to work in the Lord.

Worth more than any earthly treasures.

Fishing

You sought out the strong
fishers of men,
prolonging the goal
of a better future
laced in purple and gold.
Don't count me old,
although I have less energy
and certain types of wrinkles.
But my twinkling eyes,
such a lovely surprise.
Call me late as I am in no state
to eat the hot meal on my plate.
My stance is slightly crooked,
but my heart is not so.
No plans for dissention.
Please give me a mention.
Attentive hearts listening.
My nurturing breezes
Brought me here,
on my knees, where I can bear
what is rightfully yours.
We finished the race
embracing your face.

Follow Me

Cause for my concern:
The lantern is bright.
Come and follow me.
We will light up the night,
causing me to lift on high.
Well-lit shadows
dispersed in an instant.
Perished due to lack of belief
in our Jesus,
Who gives us relief.
Begin by calling my name.
And then your own.
Sown and brought into the picture,
measureless is our Saviour,
and loving is our neighbour,
showing us the way to go.
Reasoning and flowing,
nurtured and knowing,
the town I grew up in.
A winning formula may exist,
misshaped but still a gift.
Nevertheless, we are here.

Forget

What was it that I asked?
Passive figures apply.
Get on with the task.
Keep that twinkle.
Your eyes are good.
Your supplies will last.
The faster we go,
The slower we know.
Forgot what you said.
You wake up fresh.
Taken myself to bed.
Keep safe in your head.
The battle is won.
Keep me safe, Lord.
Should I move abroad?
Swords and daggers fly.
Not near us.
Happy by your side
when I realize
you are the one
I refuse to spar with.
Laid down and fast asleep,
she watches me when I twitch.
The itch in my conscience
leaves.
Certainly the trials

come and go,
but the grass is green.
That's all I needed to know.

Future in Your Hands

Behold the Master's plans
to unfold you
at every single hand
dealt our future grows.
Grown long enough to know
where you are.
Where do you want to grow?
Plenty of chairs to house,
plenty of mouths to feed.
Unburdened by the act
of great generosity.
Come together, we narrowly
wait.
Food we eat,
nothing left on the plate.
Clocks chime.
Time to unburden
my association with them
as they come and go.
Relief is near.
The simplistic do not feel.
Their lives are unreal.

We make our choices,
sing with our voices.
Curtain calls,
on with the show.

Guards and Nurses

Forerunners busting a gut,
trying to make their ways.
Trapped by dust and smut,
Searching for a long-stay

prison or hospital.
It's an easy choice to make.
Brutal dehumanization.
Key carriers lie in wait.

The clash, the call,
guards rushing in,
sentenced, and killed.
No sin committed.

Away with the call.
Echoes beating the walls.
Lives turned around.
Sounds of each triumph
busting down the door.

Jail or hospital?

It's built for you.
If the call comes,
be ready for the jumps,
bumps, and scars.
Reputations marred.
Come home and rest.

A new voice comes through.
'You can do it, you know.'
Hospital beds
resting our souls.
We may be aged,
But we are not old.

Head of the system

Come to me, all who are blind.
Systematic usage of the mind
searching for reality.
Far cry from the real.
But it felt real to me.
In an instant, I was drawn
to the wiles of the dawn.
When cats would come out at
night,
I was there looking for a sign.
Beginnings of a town called
home

Impostors politely controlling the zone.
What if I am one?
What should I do?
Take my foot and fit my shoe.
Belligerent   and outnumbered,
unfocused and faded.
Is the world mad?
Jaded little ones
Looking for answers,
turn to my Jesus.
He knows them all.
None too small or too big.
Crafting our escape,
it's all down on tape.

Houses

We came together
as a big family.
You can touch your toes.
It's no mystery
that you are happy,
sensing your words
coming from everywhere.
The wind is arable.
Land beyond bare.

A stable tenant
for the night.
Our King born by candlelight.
No issues there.
No need to fight.
Your rights are yours.
Sounds you have seen
no longer new to me.
Serenity we abide with.
Tenderly she waits
To come together in one big house.
Our home.

How Are You?

I was sent to bear witness
to your hope and forgiveness.
Forgetfulness has its ways
of   showering   wholesome praise.
Come back to me.
I want to see you smile.
Please come back to me.
I have waited all the while.
Seeing you for the last time.
Past hurts and pretences,
shouts and brawls.

I must have been mad
to treat you that way.
'Call me home,' I pray.
Change comes.
I no longer recognize you.
Chewing on the memories
to assert my authority.
I miss you greatly.
You are the person I was shaped
to see.
But you are gone,
And I don't know what to do.

all new and fresh.
Never second-hand gifts
from thrift shops.
Seeing you makes me curl up
in warmth,
a big ball of fuzz.
You are to me my warmth and
comfort.
My protector, my Saviour,
my all.
Thanks for listening.
Go and have a ball.
And that's not the end.

I Am Coming

You promised,
and you never lie.
Your ways are higher.
Swim with my tide.
Ride those waves,
forming and crashing the
caves.
Erosion of the coast.
But what I fear most
is hard to say.
Not lacking in words.
Wanting to add to the day.
I show ways to the Promised
Land,

I Have It All

Last but not least,
succumb to a passing feast.
A tender heart adds to my
part.
Past occurrences
yearning to ferment
the torrent and mental fight
gone now, out of sight.
Some bright spark adds the
light.
Better that way
to last through the night.
I cried that same night.

The fight is over.

Numbers went over the top,

where they should have stayed.

Taking orders is not always wise

when the leader seems wise.

But outpouring of lies

testify to the truth.

Our Jesus and our youth,

not slumbering

or breaking step or tooth.

Informer

Tell me it is real

when we are sealed with a kiss.

Found my home comforts.

Plenty miss their shots.

Commanded to us

the deliverance

out of range.

Another page of study

motioned and awakened.

Laying my love on the line,

pining for my life to see it free.

Mumbling and rumbling on

with my dedicated song,

my informer,

the man of peace,

frontlined care

and spiritual release.

Always with me,

without a care in the world.

Search me, I am here.

Please, sir, don't laugh

at my inadequacy to focus.

Out of focus but strong-willed.

The walls are cold and hard.

Still, here, though, are my thoughts.

Come to me, and feed

on the words we need to eat.

Intensity

When the dashboard is on safe,

the wind waving in your hair,

there comes a certain master

blaring out the picture or freedom.

Needless to say about the trivial,

pursuits of the rider come
to me.
Where I crossed myself,
mirrors shouted with glee.
Safety comes in on the scales.
Nails and scars and bars and
brawls
sent me to the edge of a state
where I needed to call a mate.
Impaled on a rod used to give
such protection and comfort,
intense is the word.
My birds come nesting.
They are nesters, those birds.
Fluffy, furry little beings,
where survival comes first.
Protection comes next.
Food comes after.
And chicks come to a homey
home.

It Is in You

Lay your hands on me.
Don't want to be broken.
I just want to sit
beneath the tree of life,
searching for answers,
wanting to take a wife.

Your love is in you.
Dormant.
Splashed all over me.
The one who set me free,
my hashups make me see
the wonder of you
and ponder about your ways
in a number of hazy days,
crumbled by my older waves.
Calm down, I have you made
courtesy of the One
who made the grade.
His dinner is our prayer.
His drink is our praise.
Towards him we feel.
Imagine a sense of being.
Wellness we crave.

It's Cold Out There

Nothing like some good,
fresh air.
But I will be frank.
There is no risk there.
The tank is nearly full.
I will go to all necessary
measures
to keep you in tune

with all measurable ambitions.
Because you are human,
I have to be very careful
not to risk your mind,
having too much stuff in it.
I pause for thought
when I know you are for me
and never against.
All my jolly frolicking,
testing all my medications
To the limits of my imagination.
Amalgamation stirring me up
to the point of bursting joy.
No trouble here.
Daring to be the King
of all creation and human beings.

Jazzy

I heard you say
this music makes you stray.
But in all truth,
it makes you want to stay.
Enriched with the protein
that makes grey matter dance.
Enhance your mind

with not pills but the beat.
Look at your notes.
I will make you see
that by chance, we learn
to discern our lives' protection,
our life paths.
Listen to the new generation.
It's not too much to ask.
They have the knowledge
and the freedom
to make society change.
But whatever your age,
your training comes in handy.
I'll meet you in the air.
That jazzy groove
makes me want to move
house or position.
It's your goal.
Use the ammunition
you have been given
to make new
from stagmentation.

Lasting Love

Moments where everything gels
mellow in gelatin.
Floating in a daze of comfort.
Melting in a torrent of cold.
Waves of yesterday
still causing a stir.
Burnished in golden rays,
the Son on the stage,
calm in the rage of abuse.
Possibly
quite possible to me,
is where you live in my heart.
Nothing can erase
your part in it.
I shall be with you
forevermore.
The tenderness you feel
For me cannot be stolen or taken.
Make me as you are, Jesus.
I want to feel with you.
Let us talk.
We have so much to share.

Let Me Hold You

Sitting there, I see your shape,
the way you walk and talk.
But in my mirror, I search,
but not for too long.
I know I am big.
Maybe too big for my usage,
like shifting a fridge,
shape-shifting.
But not because you are here.
It's who I am, dear,
calling out across you.
You're wild animals in the zoo
being entertainment.
Need to pay the bills, they say.
Up to my eyes in work,
I certainly am no worker.
The pleasure is mine
as I strike a pose.
Hold me now,
not out of habit.
Let us try to manage
the place we dream of.

Make Your Change

When we feel at a loss,
and you toss it into the wind,
life will come back again,
Bringing new hope and peace.
Feeling at ease with who
you are.
Carefully   trodden
adventures,
just too many to mention now.
But in time, we shall begin
to realise the strength within,
separating us from the hell
of sin.
Paths we have wandered.
No more punctures in our
tyres.
Tearing down the final
curtain.
No death for us, we are certain,
even when we feel in the
mire.
Put on me the full armour
of God.
Then we will make ourselves
understood.
My Father comes forth with
his Word
and renewed hope.

Putting on love that removes
all fear.
Nurturing me, my Father
always near.
Keep all emergency exits
clear.

Motives

Torn because of that girl,
emotional baggage
waged a war against me.
Her motive was clear—
didn't want me
but as a slave to her babble.
Rubble laid me bare,
vulnerable, and laden.
Heavy was her load.
No more.

Then there was you.
Your softness and meek nature,
stature of one,
strong like a whirlpool,
the undercurrent stripped me.
Gave me back my dignity.
My patience restored
brought me warmth,
brought me strength,

a place to be
with you next to me.
It cured me and set me free
in your loving arms
and gentle hands.
Our plans for a home
coming to fruition.
Blessings in abundance
dancing with my spirit.

My Faithful Followers

I have come to terms with—
in fact, I am certain
about my heart towards you.
No mystery now.
I have made it known.
People on the streets
say you have a home.
Curiously, I sense in you
the same qualities as my son.
In you I see a power.
The force of nature
will keep you safe from harm.
Come to me; I want to reach out,
disarm you from all malice.
No more callous actions.
A fraction of you needs care.

But generally, I will say
I think you are all there.
Wearing out your cloth,
but the moth cannot eat away
your total and utter loveliness
we are blessed to see.

My Heart's Desire

Butter me up to flutter and
mutter.
Seas swim enough to be
grounded.
Waves waving their
magnificence.
Just the right ambience.

Their moods deter me,
as do the settled way they are
searching for reason.
Girl, you have come so far.

The way you strike the bell,
the way you search for health,
minds moving into shapes.
Fortune and promise await.

Answers too much to bear.
The heart you see,

you can find answers there.
Button me up.

I sing like a canary.
Striving to be one.
Wanting the sea
but not a drop to be wet.

Feelings occur at any time,
mastered and plastered.
Much too much wine,
my ear inclined to find
a perpetual prize inside.

My Lord, My Protector

You are my umbrella
when it rains.
You are my coat
when the wind comes.
you are my sunblock
when it's too sunny.
You are my jumper
when it is cold.
You are my strength
when I am weak.
You are my confidence
when I am in doubt.

You are my skin
when I am everywhere.
You are my mind
when mine is stretched.
You are my feet
when I have no direction.
You are my lift
when I feel heavy.
You are my light
when things seem dark.
You are my touch
when I feel nothing.
You are my tears
when I sense nothing.
You are my boldness
when I am scared.
You are my safety
when I am in danger.
You are my manna
to keep me fed.
You are my tongue
when there are no words.
You are my company
when I feel alone
You are my place
when I was missing.
You are my wife
when I need kissing.

You are my reason
when I have none.
You are my child
When I need to play.
You are my green grass
when the ground is dry.
You are my teacher
when I need to learn.
You are my health
when I feel ill.
You are my ship
so I can sail the stormy seas.
You are my tip
when I have just eaten.
You are my ride
when I need to be inside.
You are my balance
when I was about to slip.
You are my grip
when I am in goal.
You are my eyes
when I struggle to see.
You are my breath
when I feel on the edge.

My Occupation

Tearing down the walls,
I see my flaws.
But I don't want to.
Carving my name,
establishing myself,
I sent you home.
Power in your frame,
your bones are strong,
And your mind is pure,
clarifying my need
for a better existence.
Sensing someone
whose loss is clear
and hard to hide,
the tides turn.
And the sandy winds burn.
But I will shelter you.
You will discern
what is right.
Come to sleep tonight.
On wings you see all
above the clouds,
sensing a change.

My Piano

Searching for your keys,
wonderfully at ease,
you know how to tease me.
Your strokes free me
from infamous tyranny.
Come and see what I will make
shaken up and made whole.
Life for you is a stroll,
and coming across an albatross
that will fly you home,
into this heart of mine.
Surely a sign from me to you.
I am yours, and you are mine,
shining for all to see.
Lovingly adored by the heavens.
November is here.
With you I will share
my preparations.
Come here, I want to tell you
your secrets.
You play wonderfully
nimble and surely fun.
My voice I give you.
You have overcome.

My Request

Further to our conversation,
I wholly recommend a station.
The fact of the matter is,
you get me ruffled
and in a tizz.
Muddled my voice
and sent it far and wide
with sentiments I cannot hide.
It's all about choice.
Caress my ears with your sweet vocality.
Start me off with good supply.
My pictures you create
in an instant camera.
Looking past my presence
but seen as in a mirror,
you come to me, swinging my door.
But I say thank you first.
Your tenderness has my name all over it.
It is a dotted relative,
bringing me good tidings,
minding your business,
get learning your lines.
it's an excellent way of life

for the wise,
for you.

My Tears

My tears have disappeared,
gone in a moment's time.
They fall away;
my eyes see why and where.
My handsome one,
keep close to me.
I will show you the peace.
I have not been hurt
by the hurting world.
They used to hurry,
jump straight in,
trying to find fault
all the time looking after
ones who sought
to buy me.
As I will show you
my perfect lines and shapes,
my light, and my saints,
certain to clear the fog.
Sleeping as a log,
I came to give life
in all its fullness.
Please take me up on my offer.

A borrowed something,
something I wanted to keep.
Weeping, I saw something
change in me.
Freedom from bondage,
a new age, a new feeling.

My Wholesome Meal

Catering for my taste,
you leave nothing to waste.
Those in love and comfort,
come over to my place,
where the birds sing.
Joys you bring
to the world.
My wholesome meal, you are
nourishing our natures.
Who are you?
To say you need a raise,
follow our Jesus,
and give our Father the
praise.
Come out of that cave,
where it is cold and dank.
It's like a sinking ship
saved from the brink.
I can give you strength,

wings upon sight.

Mighty men were lost and found.

Bound by the law,

but now see the coming of our Lord.

Opening Windows

The cold air draws in

single-minded drudgery.

Outside, the bin men work.

We look to see how they manage.

How can they work in such conditions?

Opening windows,

looking out of the system

where there are free birds,

the air is clean.

Love is in the air.

Searching for answers, we are

coming together from afar,

Talking of a long wait.

It is OK as we wake from the slumber.

Mostly there throughout the storm,

looking out in safety.

We closed the windows.

Nothing coming in

But choose what goes out.

Inside, lights bring clarity

while the wind and rain thumps.

Surely not blind,

the rivers don't mind

as we are carried home

to paradise.

Our Life

Certain to live in the day,

the question is,

Do you live that way?

Do you want to?

Come over to me,

I want to see your love.

Your eyes tell me a story.

You have come far.

What a great testimony.

Blessed to be here

in your loving arms.

Protection and a direction.

My life in accumulation

of things that mean something to me.

I am collected.
To live in your mansion,
understand me when I say
commitment to prayer.
Come see me.
I am everywhere,
sent to give life
to all who ask for it.

Our Walk

We are never alone.
Fortitude is our home.
Protected wherever we walk.
Caught above the waves,
the sand brushing our feet,
never led into defeat.
Your pleated garment
soaking up what was left.
Learning our ways,
carrying our hopes and dreams,
seemingly
steering us to a new land.
His land of milk and honey.
No need for money;
everything is free.
Taste the taste of liberty.

Come to me, and I will build
a calmness in you
that cannot be billed.
Your new best friend
is here for you
right to the end.

Outside My Window

I see you following me.
You are unaware
of my intention
to lay you down bare.
Catching you there,
bearing up, and strong.
Tenderly she kissed me.
Did I do any wrong?
Sing me the song
of the birds of the air
and the ones who care.
Come to me, all my flock.
I shall raise you up
to want more
of me, that I shall give.
Live your life.
Don't mishandle my work.
I made her for you.
Searched far and wide

with love I don't hide.
Flawless and willing,
she can do the drilling,
filling the gaps
left by its previous owner.

Picture in the Mirror

Fortified and electrified,
The gunman loses his grip.
He tried to multiply,
went on an all-night trip.
Is it true what they say,
the mirror sometimes lies?
Sent home in a crate.
What a sorry state
when a friend loses his mate.

Calm down, my friend.
Love never stops
serving the colourless.
Not out of necessity
or greed or want or need.
The heart is strong.
The beat is constant,
meant to run wild
in a forest, giving its fruit.
Tartan paint—

is it a real thing
or made out of a constant flow?
Nerves through the rain
begin to take guard.
The situation is candid,
lasting all through the seasons.
Begins to reason with
when we talk of love and honour.
The stomach cannot take the pain.
When the rain is scarce,
such a sorry place is the desert.
We get our manna
whatever the circumstance.
Spiritual food.

Prayer for John

Lord, I ask
to give John his due.
Effort he puts in,
can I say it's for you?
You fed me,
gave me a home.
I needed to be taught
right from wrong.
So I burst into song,

not to prolong your plight.
It is a long journey;
give up the fight to be right.
John, you need a home.
One inside I feel for you.
Don't bust a gut
with coarse jokes and smut.
Come to me.
I am your friend and willing
to lend you a hand.
When all is done,
your internal battle you won.
Furthermore, to request
that you lay him down to rest,
bless his heart, Lord.
His mind to follow.
No more damage or sorrow.
In your Word you say
the believer's family becomes yours,
flooring the enemy with a single blow.
My Father is here.
That's what you need to know.
Now we can grow together.
Your heart is so soft, like a pillow.
You smell of love
glorifying your name.

We are not the same.
Come with me.
You will know your name.

Rattled

In the midst of a battle,
we cry out to our Lord.
Settled in the moment,
I cry out,
saving our very selves.
This rock we have discovered,
made of strong stuff.
The spiritual being
led by faith
and not by looking
rattled the adversary
into defeat.
New clean sheets
for those who believe.
We want to be with
the Saviour of his world,
stirring up a passion.
Born into a mission,
wishing, wanting, waiting
for us to come to him.
His children, we are him,
freeing us from sin.

Relief

Tight and under pressure,
a tipple, only a small measure.
Then onward to he doesn't know where.
Bags packed and, on the run.
Again.
Let's all go home,
where it is soft,
and I'm not all alone.
Tombs beware.
There is a new kid out there,
sanctioning and sectioning.
Metal buried within
a broken body,
a fractured mind.
Strangely, healthy is his soul.
After his suffering and rough treatment,
seated at the right hand of God.
My God, ruler of the heavens and earth,
burst onto the scene.
Deserved to be first.
Appraise given to our heavenly hosts—
protectors, silencers, reactors, and dismantlers.

Rushing Waters

Come as you are.
You are no burden to me.
Striking a chord,
you sum up perfectly.
Deservedly, I say unto you,
'The power I lay in your hands
not to hurt or to choke.
I have plans to build
the blueprint I send to you.'
Draughty drafts laid under you.
We are wed in no other way
but a transmission of our Lord,
waiting for the great day
when freedom reigns.
Purposely giving way to strains.
Letting go of the failures.
Strained emotions
surrender to love.
Costly figures figured out.
What our Lord is all about,
standing on guard.
He never sleeps or slumbers.
In his care, we find our places.

Search My Heart

Wherever you find yourself,
at the back of the store,
deep shelves you hide in.
From the edge you cry out,
so you stay.
I am here, where you are.
Talk with me.
I know your pain and scars.
Come as you are.
I am your healer and guide.
I have your fortune
in my hands.
Share with me all your plans.
Bleed me; I am the giver of
life.
Drink from me as you thirst;
you would thirst no more.
Corner to corner,
you are never cornered
with you in the fight.
I am your kite to freedom,
pulling and guiding,
soaring and flowing.
Bless the wind as it pulls.
Sinless and full of love,
this kite you have presented,

sent to lighten the load.
Sewn into your flesh,
garment laid down to dress in.
Stresses of life get you down.
But I am here anyhow.

Secrecy

Words you are unable to say.
Words that make me talk
this way.
Dance with me.
I need to move and breathe.
Our secret parties,
nights in secret moments.
Torrents of giving.
Forever believing my case
for proving my place for you.
In your heart,
secret emotions overflow you.
Hidden behind your eyes,
your heart bleeds.
Flowing you in me,
sumptuous in displayed
heat,
beating the odds.
Picking up my heat,
I keep myself inside

until I feel safe in me.
It's my fortune to see.
However, you are
whatever I know.

Shake It Off

Sand dunes certainly rub
the dirt in your wound.
Stubble now rough enough
to light a match.
The sun burns;
the sweat is pouring out.
Yearning for a nice cool wind.
Friends have water and food,
but they don't bring joy.
Come over here.
I want to see you, boy.
I want to see your heart
in colour and in sync.
Another man-made man.
But I make heroes.
Towing my heavy mass,
I have to.
And you need me to
cleanse your body and mind.
I see you.
I wish to talk with you

about life, love, and what's
next.

Shattered Thoughts

Yours are clear and concise.
But mine I have to think
twice.
What do you see
when you think of me?
Courteous, grounded,
but a flighty guard?
Tough but also soft?
Wipe the sweat away.
The cloth that gives way
tenderly she says to me,
you will have to wait and see.
Blundering in and on with
life.
My woman, you shall know
tithing to family.
Please go ahead of me,
searching and knowing,
flowing   for   emotional
purposes.
Come to me, and I shall give.
Give me your life so you can
live.

Short

Sorted out into motion,
the ocean reflects his position.
Calmly walks into his mission.
Session raised my interest.
Blessings give me rest.
Kissed by the wind,
your love brings me home.
Come upon me.
I see your brilliance.
The melting pots of life,
where metals meet,
sweat relieved.
Believing the believable.
Achieving the achievable.
Surrealism and socialism
come together like a good portion
motioning towards my Maker.
Heaven-sent,
he is my Saviour.
Stopped my clamouring clamour
And mentioned my softness.
I owe it all to you.

Soft

I caught you in a daze,
weary from life's struggles
and the maze of wrong answers.
Plantation of thoughts and dreams.
Watered in essence
essentially my whole being.
Fed from the life-giving water and blood.
Misunderstood in many ways.
Waves crashing over me
As I come to see your grave.
But you weren't there.
The caves are cold and dark,
but you light up the world
away from the depressing dark.
I find myself well and fit.
The charges have been lifted.
You are free to go.
But remember this, my Son.
Some things you need to know.
As dark as this age is,
we are the lights.
We are the examples.
So watch your steps and be kind.

You also may find colour
in your cheeks and
personality.

Do not be scared of your
punctuality.

Takes a man to see what you
have seen

and still be standing.

Standing Back and Forth

My giver, I know you.

Although I tend to behold my
creation

brought from my loving
nation of peace.

Sent out the mail.

Withheld from my mind's
restraint.

Such a tall tale,

but totally true.

Kindly I say unto thee,

What caused your assurance

to faithfully approach me?

I know you are well.

I long for you to know my
mysteries.

Courteous   entertainers
thrill me.

I see you there, causing a stir.

My soul wants to be with you,

seeing what you deserve.

It's my curvy nature.

Newness of life

taught me to live,

Surely, I need to think twice.

In this maze called life, I
follow your lead,

breathing your air, and
retrieving thoughts.

Starting something

Beginnings are always tough

when you can't get enough.

Inspiration comes sparingly.

Ringleaders cut carefully.

Times ahead and already gone

forced a pressure

to prove they were wrong.

We start something

with intent to finish.

Fully finished works

that begin with a jerk.

It is the search of the mind
which

leaves us in pieces,

like the potter's wheel

sealed the edges

wedged against the finishing line.

Freedom from the race.

I take up my days

when function exists

with insistent prayer.

Major lifts and falls are minimal.

Working in shifts,

leaving the synagogue,

finding a freedom, they don't know.

Came into colour,

another victory for us.

Stepping Out in Line

I am totally convinced and sure

of my confidence in my Lord.

Called to step in line.

Under control, I did whine.

Mines and minds collide,

so I had to step out and find

a new way of life.

Taught at a young age to fight.

Battles won for me.

I know we are our Maker's delight.

Stepping out in line,

Makers modelled changes.

Surely, I found the one

to park next to me and have some fun.

Beginning to understand.

She made me into a man.

All the time following your plan.

Disarmed and disqualified

of the licence to kill,

my Lord, gloriously I shall live

in your presence and honour and love,

finding my energy from above.

Take from Me

Being your resource

to help you on your course,

take from me my failures,

and place me up on high

with you to share

reasons we are with you.

Searching you, my visionary,

how lovely it is to see

your calm philosophy.

You mainly watch and listen.
I am with you.
Your big heart glistens
through the ages,
weathering the storms,
broken free from the cages.
Amazing how we see
burdens lifted just like that.
Feeding from you,
blessing us for such trust,
covers me whole
with stardust.
My bright morning stars,
I follow you wherever you are.

where I will be,
you need to understand.
Take me on a ride,
and after, by candlelight,
show me your ways.
Oh, what a lovely sight.
Party tonight;
you are invited.
Searching you with my stare,
lovely couple over there.
Trickling slowly, come
what may.
I urge you
to be sweet; I want you to stay.

Talk about It

Chance is change.
We want it all.
Spare some coinage,
and I will show you
where it came from.
Let us talk it over.
Smother me with your
kindness.
It's not over.
He can heal your blindness.
Finding me where I am,

Talk to Me

I need to hear your voice.
Talk to me, but you do have a
choice.
You are mine, and wherever
you go,
I'm bursting out into song.
My colours live,
longing for your sparkling
eyes.
Shadowy glances come to
sight.
Come to my age.

I sense a delightful leader.

A ruler pleading for my freedom.

You know, Father, we need them.

Equal measures are a pint of pleasure.

But with you, it is always a full gift.

Giving until there is no more left.

Struggling to keep on track.

Your good deeds and heart

Make me want to come back.

They hacked me and mocked me.

Lies tried to unfold me.

But I know my Father and Maker,

and that's why I keep my cool.

And I know where I am from.

some have defected.

And I don't blame them,

as have I.

Caught in a daze,

I hear my Master.

Leg in plaster,

cast aside your angst.

Our planet needs us

to ride the tide of victory.

As a missionary, to win

the hearts and lives of everyone.

Caused and made by the Son.

Our loving Father

brought us his

heart for his people

fighting against evil.

Tardiness

March forth

in colourful display.

It was a cause

fought for our today.

Nerves a shakin' and tested.

Invested in life,

Taught to see

Believe me when I say

you are greatly loved

beyond everything

at work and at play.

The sinking feeling

seeking a break,

comforted along those lines.

Confined in space

still won't break me.
Desperately wanting a home,
forced into labour,
savouring the flavourings
of meagre givings.
Our Lord gives abundantly
to all who ask and receive.
Leaving our dwelling places
to find a new generation,
facing losses not of intention.
On a park bench,
I hope you find answers
saying unto you,
'I am watching every little
thing
you do so well in your search
for me.'
Found freedom in you.

Tension on the Mount

Case closed.
We chose to run the race
cold-nosed and grey.
Taught what you forgot.

Way up there among the stars,
trees   palming   off
responsibility.

Reasonably full and tall.
No notion passed.
Draught taken and placed
into the whirly wind,
where its home is.
We know it is shaken
By the ways of the waves,
plunging into the depths,
where the current makes a
ploy.
The ploy to change.
No longer a frivolous, dancing,
airy sky,
but a well-rounded and
peaceful lake,
where he made his home.
The higher we go,
the ride whips in and takes a
breath.
The earth standing strong,
The sea just wanting to be.

The Calling Birds

Call to me, oh lovely one,
where I ride with the Son.
Sing to me, oh beautiful lady.
Never a possible or a maybe
showing how to love her song.

My song.

Birds sing, and the peacock dances.

Come to me, my whirly girl, and we shall be the example to follow.

What about today, or rather tomorrow?

Waiting here for a melody, calling out across the meadows.

The calling birds awakened by the song of their mates.

Come over to mine.

We can stay up late, Even past eight, but come home when you are done.

Here you always have a home to roam and call your own.

The Cause

Many times I come to you.

Fortune says I must be true.

Calming my bones, I shudder to think of you with someone else.

From the brink, a casual wink,

and then you are found kissing the ground.

At least it doesn't bite back.

Returning home after getting the sack, oh, the relief;. I was free to hack into my Saturday night wardrobe.

Family never wanted for me to find my woman.

She is smart and fun.

We ran home to hers, blurring the lines between abstract and real.

She keeps me calm, and we drink fresh water.

Spoke to her at length about love, life, and what happens when you love and then walk away.

I found myself feeling astray.

Then I told myself, 'I don't walk that way.'

And there you are, arms open wide, unable to resist her amazing strength and her passionate kiss.

The Cold

It is the way you speak.
You share my hopes.
The dreams you seek
normally give homes
to the one you call your own.
Best if I say
how special you are.
Special and precious.
I wear my ring, your ring.
Singing from tree to tree.
How fortunate
I intended to be.
We serve each other
from day to night.
Polite little curtsies,
pulling faces for fun.
You are mine, girl.
Smiles and smiles.
I know your style.
No more wall prisons.
Ceiling just for show.
Come to my aid,
and you shall know it all.
It is cold out there,
but we are inside.

The County Jail

Come on and send me my mail.
This male is uncomfortably close
with his toes and clothes and all.
The clothes he keeps on
are minimal for sure.
But you can count on
his smelly allure.
Then one day I gazed at him.
His smile came through.
When I talked to his shoes.
eyes pale and wishy-washy,
I knew he needed me.
So I took this man,
taught him a thing or two,
for the ladies like shampoo.
So I cut his nails and washed his hair.
A new man he looked,
but he still had the stare.
'Come discharge,' I warned him,
'Go out and be yourself,
not behind the dirt,
but in good health.'

The Rain

Comes and blows,
but nobody knows the time
or place.
Search inside yourselves, and
find
we're not of that sort.
We are who we are,
taking a stand.
How bizarre I find you.
Ways of the wind, I hide you.
Tried and found
where my own backyard
slides into place.
Enough of the fighting.
Let us get on with the race.
Knighted at a kindly hour,
your trip today not wasted.
Less haste and less waste.
Coming up today
are our values.
You choose; it is up to you.
The rain comes,
adding up sums of control.
Waiting for it to rain again.
Place yourself in his hands.
He fights to protect us.

Our land he does not neglect.
Supple and fair,
fainting at the very sight
of his tender heart
and his majestic fight for us.

The Record shop

You store me up.
My choice incorrupt.
Taking away my revolt.
What is wrong with this?
Searching for the answer.
My answer
flicking through the leafy
leftovers.
I come across you,
the one I truly and really
want.
Dwindling
and emotionless finds.
My local record shop,
oh, what a find.
And so close.
Maybe too close.
Master craftsman finishing
my record
turns and nods.
Another record set.

Brilliant sound,
making it surely, I need not bet
because my musical needs
are met.
Number one on the charts. Sit
back in your seat.

We are the forebears
of this strange and lovely
land.
We need to look after it.
As the saying goes,
'Fit for a king.'

The Right Way

It takes strength, you know,
to go the right way.
Worth your life, many
would say.
Draw your bow.
Take a pew.
'It is finished,' he said.
Came to our rescue,
a saintly person is drawn.
Others wish they had never
been born.
Sought a place where love
rules.
It is the law,
so don't break it.
Searching for life,
make a stance.
We have come together,
hand on heart
and hand in hand,

The Rise of the Dawn

Seemingly   expansively
expanding,
meeting you for another
sight.
The fading light coming up
to the night,
Giving away its assets,
this glowing moon surfaces
to give the dawn its lasting
light.
Exchanging   its
responsibilities.
Able to decrease the heat.
Repeating the feel,
abruptly enters the stage
after a lovingly prepared
meal
eaten with my limited taste.
Consumed by haste.
You could see me
with a big smile on my face,

causing you to give the maid
a space at the table.
Able to spread the butter.
Gently passing over
passing out at the table.
Taken home to her stable.
This lady had too much to
drink.
All pretty in pink.

The search

Seeing you from afar—
a country mile—
the stars in your eyes
make me come alive.
Which came first,
the stars or the sky?
Searching for answers,
we turn to our Lord,
asking why the change
to stage or be outstayed.
To me you are bright
with colour; we are knighted.
Flight path changed due to
lack
of seeing himself in mirrors,
claiming victory over errors.

Never did say how or why.
I searched for a mentor,
but he was not in.
Then I turned to you,
asking to be let in.
You teach me.
I ask of you to teach him
wisdom,
the way to nurture.
Furthermore, I ask
to share your flask with him.
I am limited in ability,
but you are faithful,
understanding hearts and
minds.
Kind to us,
you find us flawless.
Tall are your trees.
High mountains to maintain.
Your livestock are healthy.
Your homes are built to last,
ones we don't see or build.

The shuffle

Cast your mind back
to when sense reigned
and knew no lack.

Stains removed,
gone with the wind,
knew no evil,
and sin was the past.
Control the stacks of mail
sent to the seafarers.
Do you know
what it would entail
if frailty came upon you?
The shuffle is about
not knowing what comes
next,
Fixed and born,
rejection a thing of the past.
Come with me.
We shall be
how we are made to be.
Not in secrecy.
Not elementary.
But follow the path laid.
It is your destiny.

Through the Looking Glass

What is it you see
when searching for good
company?
Do you see the sun or moon?

The glorious dawn
and the sleepy dusk
earn my attention
whenever you are there.

Are you down and frown,
sodden
taught only to learn and
swap?
If you could
in your life,
what would you swap?

In my defence, I implore
forceful desires are sore,
bearing a special baby
born of a virgin lady.
The sessions live on
in low light.

When I look at you,
you are a fine cut.
Diamonds can't compare
to your loving looks
and your head of ginger.
Looks singed by the sun.

Together We stand

Concern we cause.

Say something; don't pause.

Keep your words tight,

not wanting a discussion or fight.

Come to me

full of your delights.

Together we are reasonably happy.

Separated, we are an empty echo,

a voice in the distance

and far from home.

I taught you to live.

Don't be alone in the crowd.

Mounds of joy

pile up to the throat.

My emptiness gone,

took the right road,

the high road.

Answers implode like dynamite.

For me, it is just too much.

For peace and serenity I search.

The high mountains for love and joy.

I wish I felt love

and not just an empty toy.

Careless mumbles,

'I wish I was still a boy.'

Twenty More Days

I have seen you.

I have worked you

kept safe in the knowledge

you are my now my instrument.

To do good in this world

and in the next,

I want to keep you

for more than your time.

Timeless, you are to me

and many others.

Closer than my own brother.

We work together,

and we play together,

humbling ourselves

to be free from pride.

Take me, Lord.

Make me new.

It as if you are right with me.

But generally, you are in me,

struggling every day

to live as you preach.

My Lord, my Father, my love,
Instil in me something you
will love forever.

Unwrapped

Because we don't always see
what is inside
our friendly favours,
called in lots of flavours,
Maybe it is time for us
to keep on the path.
Cast into the sea.
Come together and find me,
and I will kindly say unto you,
'Boy, is your head screwed on?
Backwards, I believe.
Retrieve my stolen tokens,
and I shall make you King.
This land needs to bring me joy.'
Further afield, what I sense is
a decoy burst open into the air.
What happened up there?
Was it true and fair?
Come to me, and I will bring
My love's retrieval.
Sing with me until dawn,
until I find my way.

Washed Away

Could the breeze do it,
wash away my colour?
It is easy to do
when you are at home.
From the humble parts
to divine arts shown,
can't be blown away into
oblivion.
I see my Father.
He is pleased with us.
Certain to climb
the abrasive dusty sand.
Bears no resemblance
to its former figure.
Eroded lines now gone.
The song of beauty still exists,
but the wind and sand leave
no path
for us to follow.
Come to me; I will show you
what you need
to see all your elegance.
Just come to the sea,
and I shall be with you.
My certain type of menu.

Watchers

Watching as I break my record,
personal best to win by
default.

Laws are here but the ones
that fall,

ones that do no good at all.

Religion is a misunderstood
word.

Mention our Lord and his
Father,

the love who won us salvation,

It all just drifts away.

The melting pot of our faith
and ideals.

Surrealism is almost the
truth.

Battles of the mind can leave
us subdued.

Is it true? Is it real?

Read the Word in reverence.

The Holy Spirit our daily
meal.

You watch by the day,

looking for errors.

Wise companions endeavour
to bring us to the edge
and draw us back.

Take me home.

Come, holy people,
and give us what is due.
Your love and help
are the making of us.

Ways You Hold Me

Feeling you all around me,
you are certain of my ministry.
I am somewhat humbled
by your plans so great
for a young soldier boy
now in fruition.
I bring my pardon
as discussed; I should share
my all with you.
Must be mine.
What else could I do?
I claimed to be what I was not.
Come to me while I am in
range.
Show me my age,
not to destroy, but to share.
Where you go, I want to show
how dear you are.
Free me from the targets.
Wars waged, I was a misfit.
So I turned home,

into the bosom of my protector.
I humble myself further.
Not to fight, but to nurture.
Report to me your findings,
hiding away
until the final day of release.

We Are Your Saints

Come in ones or twos or more.
Jesus—our greatest ally,
sourced by our Father,
filled with his Spirit—
taught us to multiply.

Lord, your worth is beyond
compare.
We come to you prepared to
share.

Lord, we are your saints.
We came to make a point.
My Lord, you give us faith.
With oil you do anoint.

Lord, your worth is beyond
compare.
We come to you and prepare
to share.

Shake us, and make us real.
In you we have a home.
And we are sealed,
believed, and received.
In you we retrieved our hopes.

Lord, your worth is beyond
compare.
We come to you and prepare
to share.

Wearing Thin

The course I took you to,
remember I am the one
who took you in.
Am I the one who gave you joy?
Remarkable you are.
We all pitched in,
detailing your face,
describing your ways.
I would say to you,
'Watch what you taste.'
Realize I will not bend.
Send me something nice,
something new.
Don't think twice.
I hear the water is sweet,
causing me sleepy moments.

Steep hills bring me my fill
as you surfaced
from beyond.
Together we are
hand in hand.
A strong man can cause a
shift.
Shadow bearers
kept their fingers tight.
When asked for what,
simply say, 'Look to the light.'

What You Want

The curvature of tomorrow
learnt by nurturing
further and furthermore.
Sainted, my ego burst.
Humbled by adverse effects,
drawn up with the net.
Born to a family of love
above what is required.
Relinquished responsibility.
Pitied but left alone.
Mind set into a new zone,
the one you want.
His is the way to eternal life.

Crying in the centre of all
present
accentuates my emotions.
He moves and controls the
ocean.
Went on a journey to shed
blood.
Made me understand my
salvation.
Jesus is for us, not against us.
Drink the bread and wine
with us.
Show some love for our King,
who laid down his life to
bring us hope.

Where Are You?

Baking a cake of humble
beginnings.
Humble pie is what you need.
Feed me until I realize
the change you need
has to come from inside.
Come over and see me.
I have prepared a place
for you.
Beaming from ear to ear,
I understand you.
You have come far.

Come as you are.

Leave the stuff that rusts and rots,

pots and pans, crockery, and mess.

Cook me something

I want to ingest.

Bring me your love and yourself.

Personality also, even if it's a mess.

Call on me; I don't mind a protest.

Dance my name.

First and last is my Maker.

Time is a healer.

Christ is my redeemer.

Years Ago, Years You Go

At the right time,

I was brave in one eye.

Certain and true

was my responsibility to you.

Apple pies and sunrises

all looked great.

Caught me by surprise.

Your floundering waves,

smashing and crashing.

I had a good time, though.

They were never angry at me.

Just look at my teeth,

straight and well kept.

Who was I to know

that our friend called the vet,

not for me, but my caddie?

Never even knew him.

Kept just like a tabby

but bigger and certainly bold.

The cat lost consciousness

but never got old.

You're All soft

I look at you, and I sense

the craft and shape

of your every sentence.

Up to your nape in words.

Puzzles you dig up are absurd,

putting together years of history.

Oh, Father, what a mystery.

Responsibilities have to be met.

You're all so soft.

Ain't seen nothin' yet.

I feel you around me.

The gentle breeze of life
comes to my attention.
Mention the light, and see
how beautiful we are.
Come far to see me glide.
Slippery wet slide,
slipping into the water.
I found a new tenure.
Tentatively speaking and seeking.
Mention my love and believing in
never leaving your side.

Printed in the United States
by Baker & Taylor Publisher Services